CAREER PATHWAYS
IN PSYCHIATRY

CAREER PATHWAYS
IN PSYCHIATRY
Transition in Changing Times

---

edited by
Arthur Lazarus

THE ANALYTIC PRESS

1996   Hillsdale, NJ   London

Published by
The Analytic Press, Inc.
Editorial Offices: 101 West Street
            Hillsdale, NJ 07642

Typeset in Goudy by Techtype, Inc., Upper Saddle River, NJ

Library of Congress Cataloging-in-Publication Data

Career pathways in psychiatry / edited by Arthur Lazarus.
    p.   cm.
    Includes bibliographic references and index.
    ISBN 0-88163-217-1
    1. Psychiatry–Vocational guidance. 2. Psychiatry–Practice.
I. Lazarus, Arthur, 1954-
RC440.8.C345   1996
616.89'023–dc20   95-53879
                                                        CIP

Printed in the United States of America
10 9 8 7 6 5 4 3 2 1

To my mother, Lenore,
a guiding force.

To my wife, Cheryl,
a true believer.

And to my children, Joshua, Karen, Heather, and Aryn,
a continual source of inspiration.

Contents

Contributors

Bernard S. Arons, M.D. Director, Center for Mental Health Services, Department of Health and Human Services, Rockville, MD; Clinical Professor of Psychiatry, Georgetown University School of Medicine, Washington, DC.

Carl C. Bell, M.D. President and CEO, Community Mental Health Council, Chicago; Professor of Clinical Psychiatry, University of Illinois School of Medicine, Chicago.

Michael J. Bennett, M.D. Corporate Vice President for Medical Services, Merit Behavioral Care Corporation; Clinical Associate Professor of Psychiatry, Harvard Medical School, Boston, MA.

Naomi Bluestone, M.D., M.P.H. Private practice of psychiatry, Center Barnstead, NH.

Paul J. Fink, M.D. Senior Consultant, Charter Fairmount Behavioral Health System and Mustard Seed, Inc.; Vice President, InterCare Behavioral Health; Professor of Psychiatry, Temple University School of Medicine, Philadelphia; Past President, American Psychiatric Association.

M. Richard Fragala, M.D. Superintendent, Clifton T. Perkins Hospital Center, Jessup, MD; Professor of Clinical Psychiatry, Uniformed Services School of Medicine, Bethesda, MD.

Kenneth A. Kessler, M.D. President, American Psych Systems, Bethesda, MD.

Arthur Lazarus, M.D. (editor) Medical Director, Northwestern

Institute, Fort Washington, PA; Clinical Associate Professor of Psychiatry, Temple University School of Medicine, Philadelphia.

Richard J. Moldawsky, M.D.   Staff psychiatrist, Southern California Permanente Medical Group, Downey, CA.

Robert M. Post, M.D.   Chief, Biological Psychiatry Branch, National Institute of Mental Health.

Michelle B. Riba, M.D.   Clinical Assistant Professor and Director of Resident and Fellow Education, Department of Psychiatry, University of Michigan Medical Center, Ann Arbor; Vice-Chair, American Psychiatric Association Scientific Program Committee.

Arnold D. Richards, M.D.   Private practice of psychiatry, New York City; Assistant Clinical Professor of Psychiatry, New York University Medical Center, New York City.

Robert L. Sadoff, M.D.   Clinical Professor of Psychiatry, University of Pennsylvania School of Medicine, Philadelphia; Private practice of psychiatry, Jenkintown, PA.

Len Sperry, M.D., Ph.D.   Professor of Psychiatry and Director, Division of Organizational Psychiatry and Corporate Health, Medical College of Wisconsin, Milwaukee.

John A. Talbott, M.D.   Editor, *Psychiatric Services*; Professor and Chairman, Department of Psychiatry, University of Maryland School of Medicine, Baltimore; Past President, American Psychiatric Association.

Gary D. Tollefson, M.D., Ph.D.   Vice President, Lilly Research Laboratories, Indianapolis, IN.

Preface

This book explores the professional development and career choices of prominent American psychiatrists, each of whom has been identified with a particular career "track." I asked them to write a chapter that summarized their career and described how they have dealt with career transitions. My objectives were to survey modern options in psychiatry in the light of health care reform and other forces affecting clinical practice, to identify interesting career pathways in psychiatry, and to shed light on factors contributing to resistance to change. By reading about their experiences, you will be able to assess your own strengths, develop self-marketing skills, identify promising areas of practice (and some perhaps not so promising), and approach career transitions in an organized way.

Many psychiatrists have contemplated making a career change, but for one reason or another they never followed through with their plans. Recent changes in the organization and financing of behavioral health services, however, have made it compulsory for psychiatrists to reevaluate their professional standing. Fortunately, many avenues of opportunity are available to psychiatrists, both in clinical practice and outside the clinical arena. Psychiatrists in the process of making a career transition need timely and accurate information to help them evaluate alternatives and make informed decisions. In seeking such information myself, I realized how little information existed and how useful a book like this could be for trainees and psychiatrists in midcareer.

Until the 1970s, there were basically two options in psychiatry: private practice and public-sector work. Now a wide range of career pathways exists. In fact, about one-fourth of medical school graduates change their career after receiving their medical degree (Jennett et al., 1990). Among physicians who switch careers, many change their minds during residency, which is not unexpected, yet nearly one-third of physicians change their careers after entering practice. It is difficult to reconcile this finding with such statements as "Career paths for doctors do not exist. Once out of residency, a doctor is going to practice in the same specialty for the next 40 or 50 years" (Gumbiner, 1994, p. 332) and "By the time a man reaches his psychiatric residency he has already made his basic occupational choices—to enter medicine and to go into the specialty of psychiatry" (Pearlin and Klerman, 1967, p. 56). Apparently, the activities of psychiatrists have become more diverse in recent years and have reshaped the practice of clinical psychiatry (Olfson, Pincus, and Dial, 1994).

Interestingly, primary-care physicians report significantly fewer major career changes than do specialists. Although this observation is not readily explained, it has important implications for psychiatrists. The medicalization of psychiatry and the emphasis on primary care could negatively influence the choice of psychiatry as a specialty (Lee, Kaltreider, and Crouch, 1995). In contrast, gender does not appear to have a significant effect on medical career changes. Shifts in careers are usually related to changing personal interests, lifestyle issues, dissatisfaction and disillusionment with medicine, and financial and health problems (American Medical Association, 1993).

A study by the American Medical Association Council on Long Range Planning and Development identified 33 *potential* trends that are likely to occur during the next 10 to 15 years (American Medical Association, 1994). These trends include an increase in the number of group practices and integrated delivery systems; an expansion of health insurance coverage, with more care being provided by physician "extenders"; a greater role being played by businesses and a lesser role played by hospitals; increasing regulation by external agencies; and the increased use of computers and other cost-saving technologies. As financial pressures begin to limit the provision of health care services, dramatic changes in societal values could affect the patient-physician relationship and especially the provision of medical care to the very young and elderly.

Clearly, today's health care systems and the educational process that produces physicians are not the systems of 15 years ago, nor are they likely to be the systems that predominate in 10 or 15 years. Given the heterogeneity of the medical profession and the ever-changing political and socioeconomic climate, new and dynamic careers in psychiatry will surely emerge. Many are discussed in this book. This list of careers is, however, by no means exhaustive or predictive of future success. If one were to speculate about factors for success, competency, energy, and flexibility would probably be the key ingredients (Silberman, 1995).

I am grateful to each psychiatrist who has contributed highly personal information and has had the courage to share his or her innermost thoughts. These first-hand accounts are as important as, if not more important than, the facts gleaned from the research literature. There are similarities in career paths of psychiatrists, yet it is the differences that mark their chosen field and celebrate the diversity of the profession. If you can learn from these psychiatrists, you may find yourself traveling a unique pathway that leads to a rewarding career, or at least one that avoids the many pitfalls along the way. *Bon voyage!*

REFERENCES

American Medical Association (1993), *Leaving the Bedside: The Search for a Non-Clinical Medical Career.* Chicago: American Medical Association.

American Medical Association (1994), *The Future of Medical Practice.* Chicago: American Medical Association.

Gumbiner, R. (1994), Prospectives of an HMO leader. *Inquiry,* 31:330–333.

Jennett, P. A., Kishinevsky, M., Bryant, H., & Hunter, K. L. (1990), Major changes in medical careers following medical school graduation: When, how often, and why. *Acad. Med.,* 65:48–49.

Lee, E. K., Kaltreider, N., & Crouch, J. (1995), Pilot study of current factors influencing the choice of psychiatry as a specialty. *Amer. J. Psychiat.,* 152:1066–1069.

Olfson, M., Pincus, H.A., & Dial T. H. (1994), Professional practice patterns of U.S. psychiatrists. *Amer. J. Psychiat.,* 151:89–95.

Pearlin, L. I. & Klerman, G. L. (1966), Career preferences of psychiatric residents. *Psychiat.*, 29:56–66.

Silberman, E. K. (1995), Successful psychiatric practice in the present and future. In: *Successful Psychiatric Practice: Current Dilemmas, Choices, and Solutions*, ed. E. K. Silberman. Washington, DC: American Psychiatric Press, pp. 203–210.

❋ 1 ❋

From Public Health Physician to Private Practitioner

[PRIVATE PRACTICE]

Naomi Bluestone

Dr. Bluestone is in the solo practice of psychiatry in a small town in New Hampshire. Psychiatry is her second career. Board Certified in Public Health and Preventive Medicine, she was formerly Associate Clinical Professor of Community Medicine at the Albert Einstein College of Medicine of Yeshiva University, New York City, and Assistant Commissioner for Chronic and Long Term Care, City of New York Department of Health. Dr. Bluestone, until very recently a consulting editor of the *New York State Journal of Medicine*, is also a nationally known medical writer and the author of almost 200 articles on social medicine and psychiatry. Her book, *So You Want to Be a Doctor: The Realities of Pursuing Medicine as a Career* was selected one of the 40 best books of the year by *School Library Journal* when it was published. She is an alumna member of Phi Beta Kappa and Alpha Omega Alpha, the honor medical society. Dr. Bluestone has also been a member of the Physicians Forum, The Medical Committee for Human Rights, Physicians for Social Responsibility, and Physicians for a National Health Insurance Program.

Let me begin by telling you that, in choosing the private practice of psychiatry, I did everything backwards. So it is fitting that I write this when all of medicine, especially the private practice of psychiatry, is being turned upside down. Let me give you some of my background so you can understand my thoughts on the pros and cons of private practice.

1

SOCIAL MEDICINE

When I completed my rotating internship at Albert Einstein Medical Center in Philadelphia in 1963, my classmates were stampeding into specialty and subspecialty training, with an eye to prestige, big bucks, and collegial dinners at the homes of their mentors. Still exhausted from a relentless postmono syndrome, however, I viewed the prospect of three more years of "36 on, 12 off" as a medically sanctioned, clinically updated version of the Bataan Death March. Instead, I decided to blaze a trail and follow my major interest, an ambiguous and dubious concept not legitimized by board certification, known vaguely as "social medicine."

I came by this decision honestly, having been raised in a home where the concept of social justice and the individual's duty to the community were of driving importance. My father, a dentist turned social worker, was the director of a community agency, and so our philosophical discussions at home often centered on when and under what circumstances the pursuit of individual growth and happiness should bow to the greater good of maintaining a stable society. How ironic that this has become the key issue of our time!

Among my large family of 20 or more physicians, my senior uncle had forsaken private practice with that very purpose in mind – to use medicine as an instrument of social justice. A hospital administrator, he was founder of our modern concept of home care, an early advocate and initiator of prepaid group practice, and the first to develop a paid, full-time medical staff (at Montefiore Hospital in New York City). He greatly encouraged me to pursue a career in which the patient was the community itself.

I obtained a master's degree in public health at the University of Michigan, where I was fortunate to be one of the earliest students of the great theoretician of evaluating the quality of medical care, Dr. Avedis Donabedian. My graduate work was followed by a residency in Public Health at the City of New York Department of Health. At that time, it was a mecca that attracted mature students from every corner of the globe. Medicaid had just become a reality, and my job was to bludgeon improved quality from participating hospitals in return for a higher fee for clinic visits; I did it by starting a new organization, the New York Association for Ambulatory Care, now in its 30th year.

Becoming certified in preventive medicine and public health, I went on to a variety of interesting, relatively low-salaried positions in my chosen field. I did academic work and administration at Mt. Sinai Hospital in New York, which had just opened its medical school, and developed a long-standing intolerance for the arrogance of academic excellence in the process. I went to India to visit a classmate from Michigan and returned so ill I had to interrupt my career to work for three years at Manhattan State Hospital as a general physician, grateful for the fairly lax standards of accountability which enabled me to recuperate and still bring home a paycheck. Taking care of 200 deteriorated, senile "grannies," I never again saw a nursing home with the eyes of innocence. I also learned the limitations of the press as an instrument of change: my exposé of the wretched conditions in the hospital on the Op-Ed page of *The New York Times* was met with an expert whitewash and cover-up. I was hosed away, and the abuse continued. At the time, I never figured to become a psychiatrist.

I did a stint as Director of Community Medicine at Bird S. Coler Hospital for the chronically ill, where the handicapped, long-term sick, and other orphans of medical interest were tended. Then, at the invitation of the Health Commissioner, Dr. Lowell E. Bellin, who liked the articles I was writing, I went back to Worth Street, this time as Assistant Commissioner for Chronic and Long Term Care. Despite the hard times—I arrived coincident with a major fiscal crisis that necessitated mass lay-offs—I found time to enjoy the excitement of public administration in the Big Apple. I'm ashamed to admit what fun it was to be a big shot, have a car and a driver, be pursued by important people, and give entertaining speeches for black tie health care fund raisers at the Waldorf-Astoria. Never before or since have I been so well dressed, so sought after! It was a major educational experience for me and made me forever distrust people in power, including myself. The Health Department also taught me my street smarts: I don't make the mistake of traveling to a meeting across town without calling first to make sure it's still on, and I play the old Army/Navy game like a pro, never showing up with fewer people than the opposition. Public administration is a far cry from the solitude of a private office!

My last position before reevaluating my professional life completed some sort of internal circle for me. Not heeding dire precautions that "teaching is the last resort of the burned out," I went to Montefiore Hospital, now a major medical center, to see if I could teach residents in "social medicine" some of the things I'd learned. It was a miserable failure, for I was basically a middle-class Jewish liberal with intellectual tastes, thrown to a pack of radical ("Zionism is Racism"), rigidly humorless young hold-overs from the 60s. They ate me for breakfast.

A SECOND CAREER

The decision to return to one-on-one patient care was complex. I still valued the public good but had grown tired of losing my job every time the mayor conceded an election, a superior officer got a promotion and left me to scramble for a new spot, or political opponents started screaming. For the first time, I found myself wanting to be my own boss, to make my own hours and be accountable only to my conscience. Like Scarlett clutching a fistful of Tara, I swore I would never work for anyone else again. In retrospect, how ironic that I should choose the private practice of psychiatry just as it was going up in flames, like the South during Sherman's march to the sea!

It took me almost 20 years, that statistical norm for second-residency physicians, to return to clinical medicine. I did it because caring for the community now seemed like a hopeless task, and I was ready to give up my grandiosity and return to exploring the individual. This was exciting, for there had always been ambivalence and guilt about not using my hard-won clinical skills. I never forgot what I had gone through to become a doctor back in the 50s. (In those days, women trying to become physicians were routinely brushed off the coats of admission committees like annoying pieces of lint.) Now I was to become a *real* doctor again! You can imagine my dismay to discover that the only physicians more ridiculed and put down than public health physicians are psychiatrists! Like a hopelessly messed up omelet, I had gone from the frying pan to the fire.

While I was correct in believing that my affinity for psychiatry and the ease with which a psychiatric office could be established would make it the most practical choice for a returning physician, I severely underestimated the extent of clinical and research advances that had been made during my years in the bureaucracy. It had become a biologically based specialty, and catching up was difficult. It helped to be motivated by the opportunity to make a little money. By now I knew how much it would take to keep me in a nursing home after my own Alzheimer's set in.

I did my psych residency when I was 43. Except for the nights on-call, it was fun, an opinion not shared by my superiors, as I was in no mood to tolerate the usual exploitation of the pecking order and urged fellow residents not to either. The first year was spent at Creedmoor Psychiatric Center. It was a good experience in "community psychiatry" and interesting to work with schizophrenic patients, particularly those classic cases who write their own mysterious language and speak it with such poetic eloquence. When a second-year position opened at nearby North Shore University Hospital, a Cornell affiliate, a transfer was possible, and I had the opportunity to learn another kind of psychiatry, the character disorders and classic outpatient therapy. Psychotherapy was no longer a requirement for a residency, which I think was a great loss. In any case, I had undergone a lengthy analysis some years before, with two much loved and guiding lights in my life. (Both of them, Dr. Simon Grolnick and Dr. Edith Jacobson, are now deceased, and the psychiatric world is much diminished.)

I opened my office even before my residency was completed. My architect husband designed a small office for me behind the garage of our home in Great Neck, New York, and I never had to commute to work again. I could make my own hours and see patients whenever it was mutually convenient. Because I had advanced typing and clerical skills, I did not need a secretary or any other staff. An answering machine and a typewriter, and later a computer, made me completely self-sufficient. I had virtually no overhead, since even the heat in the office was "run-off" from the house. I started to draw income from this affluent community. When my practice was professionally appraised a few years after I began, we were amazed to discover that my collection rate was well over 98%, a fact that I attributed to my taking up dereliction in payments as a therapeutic issue with patients. Zoning that permitted home employment was helpful. Even my husband was able to practice out of the guest wing upstairs, permitting both of us to live and work under one roof at minimal expense. Between the two of us, we saved at least $1,000 a month by not needing to rent office space in our pricey town. Best of all, we could even sneak out together for a luncheon special at the local hang out!

Six years after my practice opened, my husband and I sold our home and relocated to our country place at Suncook Lake, on a dirt road in central New Hampshire. The antique farmhouse had been meticulously restored and "historically modernized" over a period of years, and, with the addition of a modern, four-bay garage with office space overhead, we were ready to resume a rural equivalent of our urban practice style. Colleagues thought we were nuts to give up our thriving practices, but we were always risk takers. The transitions went without a hitch, and now I can report on over 10 years of experience with the solo private practice of psychiatry.

RURAL PRACTICE

For the first few years of practice, being a psychiatrist was a joy. I felt privileged to hear the deepest thoughts of those in trouble, listened carefully, kept my mind going a mile a minute, was never bored, and always felt I was doing something to help. Particularly in the rural practice, I was able to see and treat all kinds of pathology that in urban centers would have had to be referred to specialists in child or geriatric psychiatry, for example. What more can a physician ask? The only problem I could identify was having to sit like a lump all day and get fat and out of shape. Also, it was a nuisance and an expense to purchase benefits like health and malpractice insurance, available to salaried physicians as perks. Nevertheless, professionally all went well, in sync with what I had been taught and how other reputable physicians were practicing. The winds of change were still somewhere off shore.

All this now seems a lost world. The rapid dissolution of private practice as we knew it has rendered my experience, in fact that of my entire generation, oddly unhelpful to those entering private practice today.

On the surface, my practice still runs as before. I see patients on the hour for 45 to 50 minutes, some for twice-a-week therapy, some for weekly "show and tell" talks. Some patients come for quick medication checks, some for couples or family intervention. All found me much more comfortable with the new psychopharmacology than the old timers would have believed possible. I have adapted, used short-term therapies with some patients, and learned to laugh at some of my old psychodynamic interpretations, particularly when the symptoms vanished with Prozac. Although by choice unaffiliated, I grab rounds at the local teaching hospital whenever possible and keep up my continuing medication education. Yes, all would seem well. But I am on the way out, and I know it.

My impending fadeaway, like that of the old soldier, comes at a time when the need for psychiatrists is growing, for this country is in deep trouble, and people no longer turn to religion for relief of the inevitable pain of being human. In suburbia, we see diseases of wealth; in the country, the diseases of poverty. But human misery is human misery, no matter what the source. And people are still willing to come, to pay what they can, and to work hard to feel better.

This is true particularly of women, by the way, who want women to talk to and selectively seek them out. I am the only woman psychiatrist in a 25-mile radius. I do no advertising, am not listed in the yellow pages, and keep a low profile, but my practice is as full as I can handle. In fact, I would be swamped if I did not exert controls. People come by word of mouth, are referred by local physicians, or take great trouble to find me. But soon they will not find me anymore. Why is this? It will not be because, like most psychiatrists, I have gone back to urban living, where culture, good food, higher fees, and heterogeneous populations abound. It will be because I do not have what it takes to put up with the abuse that is becoming routine for private solo practitioners.

AN ENDANGERED SPECIES

Everywhere one hears dire predictions about the transitional, isolated, often unaffiliated, office-based private psychiatrist, who generally does long-term psychotherapy or psychoanalysis, with or without the use of medication. For too long, it is said, he has practiced an antiquated, theory-based talk treatment that is now being invalidated, and is replaceable by shorter, time-limited interventions and ever more refined psychotropic agents. Since change comes very slowly, often by attrition, we will have to tolerate these old fogies a bit longer, but, sooner or later, their cost-inefficient mumbo-jumbo will go the way of the typewriter, the slide rule, and the Atcheson, Topeka, and Santa Fe. Whenever I hear this kind of talk, I quake in my boots, because it is *me* they are talking about. And I don't want to go belly up.

Perhaps it is premature to say that independent doctors who see patients, give them their best, and then sleep well at night are a doomed species. But their habitat is clearly being destroyed. They are being asked to adapt to changes in practice that are often inconsistent with their professional knowledge, training, standards, and ethics. Private practitioners are hounded from pillar to post, driven to distraction by the insatiable demands of the corporate world that now consumes them. No wonder they are always on the defensive! It was bad enough when all they had to deal with were deadbeats, missed appointments, multiple insurance companies, triplicate forms, unlimited bureaucratic snafus, and other coronary-causing agita. Now they must rub elbows not only with the insurance companies but their managed care entities as well, neither of whom seem to talk to each other, much less to the doctor. A whole army of office staff can't spare them the paperwork and information crunching that only they can do. Their phone calls are placed "on hold" for up to 20 minutes while they listen to canned music no one should be subjected to, and when their ears are calcified they're insulted by surly reviewers with a fraction of their education.

The private psychiatrist is under pressure at every turn to conform to preset standards devised to protect someone else's bottom line, all of which interfere directly or indirectly with his decision making. When he rebels against these thoroughly unwarranted intrusions into the practice of medicine, he is accused of being recalcitrant, self-serving, greedy, and profligate with scarce resources. If he doesn't play ball, he gets kicked out of the game. The final indignity is that all around him he sees people growing wealthy from layer upon layer of middle management. Cost consciousness does not appear to extend to the salaries and perks of those who ride herd on the physician.

The private psychiatrist functions without the backup of a large institution, a safe haven to which one becomes accustomed after years of training. There are howling wolves out there in the wild, and the physician who tries to run his own course encounters the traps of many hunters. He is often asked to release the kind of personal information that is usually given to no one but a priest, the IRS, or a blackmailer. He is forced to plead for necessary services for patients and then is treated as if he were seeking special favors for his own mother. We all have had lengthy appeals denied by fellow physicians who literally read our justification for the first time as we are talking on the phone and invariably base their approval of hospitalization solely on whether or not the patient is suicidal or homicidal. They make ME homicidal! And my malpractice rates were just raised again.

MANAGED CARE MENTALITY

The matter does not end there. You would be wise to accept that much of the intellectual base of "managed care" is totally idiotic. Case in point. I once treated a single, Roman Catholic, Irish engineer with a number of unmarried sibs, for psychogenic impotence. His treatment was routinely challenged by his managed care company. I was roundly criticized for not expressing my treatment plan in the style and jargon of the management boys I had left behind at the Health Department. My treatment goals, I was told by the licensed but not graduate-trained social worker by telephone, should have been expressed as follows: "As a result of treatment (six to eight sessions), the patient will be able to have intercourse three to five times a week". ("Oh, lady," I thought, "From your mouth to God's ears!") I then asked this young woman what would happen if I should fail to cure my man in the foreordained amount of time. "Well," she said, "You should write down something like, 'The patient is still unable to have intercourse, but now he doesn't feel so bad about it!'" (She then went on gratuitously to offer that I sounded a little hostile, so there would be no point in discussing the case further. Well, at least she got one thing right.) If this surrealistic interchange makes absolutely no sense to you, spare yourself and don't go into private practice!

I think I speak for all private practitioners who have not yet been coopted by the new system when I say that it beats me how society expects physicians to behave in an ethical, autonomous, inner-directed way and then treats them like potential malefactors at every turn. If you can't trust someone with a medical license to make a medical decision, why give him a license? If the practitioner won't conform to reasonable requests concerning "won't-go-away" issues such as cost control, why not monitor or educate him in some way and leave the rest of us alone? If you can't trust a doctor to continue his medical education because it's the proper thing to do, why charge him $20.00 a credit (x 20 credits annually) for a symposium he's going to sleep through anyway? If a doctor believes he does best working alone and not as part of a humongous panel system, why can't the system accommodate him? And, worst of all, if your doctor is nothing but a fox in a hen house, why send a chicken to guard him? Of course, we know the answers to these questions. Managed care companies do not want psychiatrists in private practice and have adopted many tactics to clean them out.

THE FUTURE

I do not know what changes will be made in the health care system in the near future. I can only trust, as an optimist, that pervasive issues such as those I am voicing here will be addressed. At the present time, however, I have reluctantly come to the conclusion that *it is virtually impossible for a psychiatrist to practice ethically in the current climate.* Under the ubiquitous influence of managed care, we are called on to make decisions that, in a subtle, barely perceptible way, undermine and erode virtually everything we believe in. Each day it seems that a goodly chunk of the intellectual and moral base, in fact the whole civilized substrate on which medicine has been practiced, is being tossed out wholesale. It is downright harrowing to see long-established networks of patient care that *worked* being systematically dismantled by the changing system. We are forced into a "If you can't beat 'em, join 'em" posture, when neither alternative seems acceptable. This is a recipe for psychosomatic or stress-related illness. If I thought it would do any good, I'd go right out and get one.

Doctors who in the past would have stayed in private practice until their 80s do seem to be retiring much earlier. Many of those who remain do so because they still have to get three kids through college. The retreating hordes search frantically for other occupations to keep their income alive, prepping for alternative careers till the wee hours.

Those who saw the handwriting on the wall several years ago have sewn up all available managerial and other salaried appointments. Others must now scramble.

In fairness, the phenomenon is common to all in private practice, not just psychiatrists. My husband's physician is in graduate school. My physician edits a medical journal. One acquaintance is in a physician administration program, trying to be one more chief in a profession with fewer and fewer Indians. Another is a reviewer for a managed care company; at professional parties, she can no longer hold her head up, being perceived as having joined the enemy. But with young children, what choices does she have? More and more restaurants are being purchased. I myself am thinking seriously of raising aquatic plants on our lake, in the hope that water lilies may contain some unknown therapeutic chemical! Most middle-aged psychiatrists, however, are stuck and have nowhere to go. So they plod on.

I am told there is a new breed of psychiatrist coming up who doesn't mind being monitored up the gazoo, keeping regular hours so he can have "quality time" with his family, or making less money despite his educational debts. He will readily adapt to being part of a huge series of networks because he has never experienced the satisfaction of being his own boss. He will thrive on multiple panels and scoot around the various bear traps which this professional life style entails. Because he has never been in analysis, or has only had "short-term" psychotherapy, he has no sense of what self-knowledge and interpersonal skills he has lost in the mad rush to embrace the heady field of psychopharmacology. (Alas, these are skills he will need when the highly touted meds leave one third of all patients dumped right back in the physician's lap somewhat worse for their clinical trials.) He has never known anything better, I'm told, and so he will carry on. If this is true, I don't know whether to laugh or cry.

Opinion is divided on what the outcome of the revolution in the structure of medicine will be. Some say it will crash of its own weight in five to fifty years. Some feel that the old order, whatever that means, will never return. For private practitioners, if they continue to exist, the issue will not be payment mechanisms (capitation, private fees, etc.). It will not be the structure of practice (solo practitioner versus group practice, open versus closed panel, etc.). Nor will the issue be the appropriate use of new knowledge in genetics, technology, pharmacology, or techniques of psychotherapy. The issue will be the quality of care a private practitioner will be permitted to give, care that is ethically, morally, and psychologically acceptable to a good doctor who wants to give the best.

My best advice to those planning a career in private practice is to be prepared for a hard reading of the small print.

RECOMMENDED READING

Bluestone, N. (1993), Psychic advisor. NY State J. Med., 1:50–53.

Knesper, D. J., Belcher, B. E., & Cross, J. G. (1989), A market analysis comparing the practices of psychiatrists and psychologists. Arch. Gen. Psychiat., 46:305–314.

Lazarus, A. (1995), Preparing for practice in an era of managed competition. Psychiat. Serv., 46:184–185.

Mogul, K. M. & Rubin, J. E. V. (1995), Private practice. In: Career Planning for Psychiatrists, eds. K. M. Mogul & L. J. Dickstein. Washington, DC: American Psychiatric Press, pp. 91–102.

Olfson, M., Klerman, G. L., & Pincus, H. A. (1993), The roles of psychiatrists in organized outpatient mental health settings. Amer. J. Psychiat., 150:625–631.

Silberman, E. K., ed., (1995), Successful Psychiatric Practice: Current Dilemmas, Choices, and Solutions. Washington, DC: American Psychiatric Press.

2

Psychoanalysis: A Personal Odyssey

[PSYCHOANALYSIS]

Arnold D. Richards

Arnold D. Richards, M.D. is Training and Supervising Analyst at the New York Psychoanalytic Institute and Assistant Clinical Professor of Psychiatry at New York University Medical Center. Formerly editor of *The American Psychoanalyst,* he is currently editor of the *Journal of the American Psychoanalytic Association.* Dr. Richards has contributed more than 70 articles and book chapters to the psychoanalytic literature and is coeditor of two volumes, *Psychoanalysis: The Science of Mental Conflict — Essays in Honor of Charles Brenner* (The Analytic Press, 1986) and *Fantasy, Myth, and Reality: Essays in Honor of Jacob A. Arlow* (International Universities Press, 1989). He is a member of the New York Psychoanalytic Society, the American Psychoanalytic Association, the International Psychoanalytical Association, and the Psychoanalysis Division of the American Psychological Association.

OUT OF AN ANALYST'S PAST

Not surprisingly, my personal route to psychoanalysis goes back to childhood. My earliest lexical memory is of reading about the death of Sigmund Freud in 1939 in the Yiddish *Forward* when I was five years old. I remember the picture of the man with the beard, and the large announcement of his death that was first read to me by a grandfatherly figure who also had a beard and who taught me to read Yiddish and Hebrew. Before I reached adolescence, I had read about Freud in the encyclopedia and pursued some of the topics described there as part of my broader search for sexual knowledge. In retrospect, it is difficult to determine whether my interest in sexuality fueled my interest in literature or whether it was the other way around. But I do remember reading novels by authors like Pearl Buck and Aldous Huxley both for their literary and for their titillating value.

The first important piece of nonfiction that I read was Flanders Dunbar's work, *Emotions and Bodily Health*. I was then about twelve and a half, and my interest in the book was stirred by my yearly bout with hay fever, from the middle of August to the end of September, and a less dramatic case of rose fever during the spring. In the preautumnal period, I felt as if I were literally drowning in a sea of secretions from the depths of my mucous membranes. Dunbar's book made the case that allergies, asthma, and hay fever were psychosomatic, somehow connected to the passions of my child's mind. Conflict, sexuality, and the unconscious were concepts that offered me the hope of mastery, a power over my membranes that came from understanding how the mind worked and how the mind in its workings affected the workings of the body.

Some four years separated my reading Flanders Dunbar and Freud's *New Introductory Lectures of Psychoanalysis* in the old yellow permaback edition. I found Freud's interlocutory style in these lectures absolutely convincing. The concepts of psychic determinism, unconscious mental processes, and infantile sexuality offered a way to order the mysterious world of mind and human interaction—mind at work and mind at play, mind during the day and mind at night—that simply brooked no competition. Freud's *Introductory Lectures* and *Interpretation of Dreams*, in A. A. Brill's early translations, formed a foundational pair; they represented a solid psychology that could be applied to early functioning and to the world of pathology.

Starting from this point, psychoanalysis became a lens through which I observed a whole host of intellectual, literary, and scientific experiences. It served a role similar to that of Marxism for others of my generation. Whether I was reading T. S. Eliot, e. e. cummings, Homer, Aeschylus, or Euripedes in high school; Aristotle, Plato, or Kant at the University of Chicago; or works on neurophysiology and brain functioning in medical school, psychoanalysis offered relevant organizing principles. Through it, I could understand a broad range of intellectual movements that I read about during the day; it likewise helped me parse the dreams I had at night.

Although I nearly succumbed to the lure of a New York psychiatric residency program that was almost totally identified with analysis, I opted for a residency at the Menninger Clinic in Topeka, Kansas, which, while analytically oriented, was much broader in overall outlook. There I benefited greatly from exposure to some of the great minds of our century—Konrad Lorenz, Aldous Huxley, S. Y. Hayakawa, Margaret Mead, and Ludwig von Bertolanffy, among others. In Topeka, as in Chicago during my college days, my emphasis was on trying to place psychoanalysis as science and intellectual discipline within the broad context of Western humanistic and scientific thought. When I began analytic training at the New York Psychoanalytic Institute in 1964, I brought to that rather rarified atmosphere a sense of the broader scientific landscape—or so I like to think. At the same time, I had the personal sense that psychoanalysis, as an investigative and explanatory tool, contained a set of explanatory constructs of awesome power; I refer to the Oedipus complex, infantile sexuality, the dynamic unconscious, and the place of love and hate in human nature.

My analytic class began as a group of 12 psychiatrists and one psychologist, 12 men and one woman. We were convinced that our training would bring us to the top of the psychiatric profession and provide us with the most therapeutically effective tools for relieving human psychological suffering. We were awed by instructors who were among the great figures of contemporary analysis. Several had a direct lineage from Freud, had been transplanted from Vienna not so long ago, and were authors of the definitive works in the field. I refer to Heinz Hartmann, Rudolph Lowenstein, Edith Jacobson, Annie Reich, Kurt and Ruth Eissler, and George Gero. And there was a group of American analysts, somewhat younger, but also giants in the field: Phyllis Greenacre, Jack Arlow, Charles Brenner, David Beres, and Martin Wangh. This latter group of analysts, joined by Leo Rangell on the West Coast, were the principal architects of what has become the modern structural viewpoint. Building on Freud's theory of the three psychic "agencies" or "structures" of id, ego, and superego, these analysts developed the notion of psychoanalysis as a psychology of conflict. According to this viewpoint, psychoanalysis approaches mental life from the standpoint of intrapsychic forces in conflict and the compromises that are the outcome of such conflict. Modern structural theory has progressively refined and amended Freud's hypothesis in the interest of achieving a better theoretical understanding of the meaning of conflict, a fuller appreciation of the range of conflicts and compromise formations, and a more powerful clinical approach to the psychoanalytic treatment of such conflicts.

With so distinguished a faculty, the New York Psychoanalytic Institute was conducive to idealization, identification, and acceptance of theory and ideology. It was hardly a place that promoted skepticism, questioning, and argument, although several members of my class did develop a skeptical posture and ended up leaving the program. Of course, at the same time that an analytic candidate attends classes, he or she is also undergoing a training analysis and probably will stay the course depending on whether or not that experience is positive. After all, what is taught always stands or falls not as hypothetical, but on the extent to which the constructs are true to personal experience.

My own training analysis was true to my experience, and I emerged from analytic training with understanding and conviction about what I consider the central tenets of analysis. I readily acknowledge that others might view differently what is central to the field. But let me briefly summarize the core concepts that I learned or had significantly reinforced during training. These fundamental tenets have to do with: (1) the basic principle of psychic determinism; (2) the centrality of unconscious mental functioning and its implications for our theories of motivation, symptom formation, personality disorder, and personality development; (3) the ambivalence and conflicts of childhood and the centrality of experiences with parents and siblings; (4) the centrality of bodily process and the human tendency to shrink from giving such bodily processes a central role in the development of personality and psychopathology; (5) the role of transference as a vehicle for bringing the central childhood conflicts into the therapeutic arena where they can be studied and altered; and (6) the centrality of affect—that analysis is a psychology of emotionality and not just an intellectual discipline.

THEN AND NOW

The period of my psychiatric and analytic training was the heyday of psychoanalysis. Following World War II, a cohort of psychiatrists returned from their wartime experience and sought analytic training. During the 50s and 60s, the American Psychoanalytic Association grew rapidly, training institutes had many applicants, and treatment centers had large backlogs. As a profession, analysis seemed to provide for the intellectual, therapeutic, and socioeconomic needs of a generation of psychiatrists who were ambivalent about the medical profession owing to its trade-school aspects and seeming lack of intellectual excitement.

Even during this era of "the psychoanalysis of plenty"—plenty of candidates, plenty of patients, and plenty of prestige for analysts—change was in the air. In the decade following the war, analysts began to write about the widening scope of analysis, exploring the degree to which, and the ways in which, the analytic method could be adapted to the treatment of sicker patients. During the course of my training, it seemed that the scope had already widened, with the so-called ideal analytic patient—cooperative, neurotic, lacking serious psychopathology—already being the exception rather than the rule. Coterminous with debate about the scope of analytic treatment was the birth of modern object relations theory as a distinct psychoanalytic school of thought. Pioneered by British theorists like Melanie Klein, D. W. Winnicott, and W. R. D. Fairbairn, object relations theory deemphasized Freud's notion of biologically grounded drives while stressing issues of bonding and attachment, especially between the infant and its mother. According to this viewpoint, it is not unconscious fantasies per se that are pathogenic, but early patterns of interaction with significant objects (mother, father, siblings) that are established early in life and subsequently internalized. In this country, Margaret Mahler's pioneering observational research with infants and toddlers, which led to her delineation of the series of stages through which psychological separation from the mother is achieved (her "separation-individuation process"), was an influential variant of the object-relations approach.

In the 60s, clinical preoccupation with the widening scope gave way to animated debate about the status of psychoanalytic metapsychology. A group of analysts, primarily students of David Rapaport, forcefully questioned Freud's metapsychology, in particular its assumptions about "psychic energy." Theorists like George Klein, Merton Gill, and Roy Schafer argued that analysis was a clinical theory and that Freud's metapsychology was at best superfluous and at worst misleading. The antimetapsychology movement continues to the present time.

Drawing on foundations provided by the proponents of the "widening scope" and by the critics of metapsychology, psychoanalysis has grown over the past quarter-century into a pluralistic movement of competing schools of thought. This trend first emerged in the 70s, following the publication of Heinz Kohut's *The Analysis of the Self* (1971) and *The Restoration of the Self* (1977). Kohut represented the first serious challenge to classical analysis; his "psychology of the self" offered a new theory of pathogenesis and a new theory of treatment and cure. According to this theory, pathology betokens the failure, in early life, to achieve a vital, cohesive "nuclear self," and this failure, in turn, is generally rooted in unempathic, unresponsive mothering that has not mirrored and reinforced those early feelings of grandiosity that blossom into healthy feelings of vitality and self-worth.

Kohut was not alone in offering the self as the umbrella for a new psychoanalytic paradigm, but he alone gained widespread recognition that, by the early 80s, formed the basis of a new psychoanalytic movement. Why was this the case? Kohut's rhetoric was engaging, and his book offered a serious challenge to the received psychoanalytic wisdom of the time. He offered an appealing dichotomy of "Guilty Man" and "Tragic Man," the former's problems originating in intrapsychic conflict (the neurotics of Freud's day) and the latter's primarily from developmental arrest and a resulting lack of cohesion and vitality in the self (the narcissistically disturbed patients of the present).

Over the past decade, self psychology has been on the wane as the flash point of psychoanalytic controversy. It has been supplanted by newer relational, interpersonal, and intersubjective schools of thought. And outside the U.S., Kleinian psychoanalysis (following the approach of the British analyst Melanie Klein), Lacanian psychoanalysis (following the approach of the French analyst Jacques Lacan), and object relations psychoanalysis (following the contributions of the British school and of Americans like Otto Kernberg) continue to have strong followings. Given the theoretical pluralism in the field, it is hardly surprising that one important task of recent years has been to delineate the clinical "common ground" that links analysts of different orientations (Wallerstein, 1992).

I myself remain a contemporary Freudian analyst with a strong belief in the central role of conflict, compromise formation, and unconscious fantasy in psychic life and in psychopathology. Over the past two decades, my writing has involved discussions and critiques of many of the newer approaches summarized above. I have been appreciative of the insights provided by these approaches, but critical of their selective emphases (whether on subjectively reported self-states, patterns of interaction, or intersecting intersubjectic worlds) and resulting devaluation of unconscious intrapsychic conflict. Yet I have enjoyed, and have benefited from, my dialogue with analysts of different stripes and persuasions. I am especially fortunate to have had opportunities for interaction with nonmedical analysts to a greater extent than many of my medical colleagues have enjoyed. This follows, no doubt, from my eclectic interests, my psychiatric training at the Menninger Clinic, and my being married to a psychologist-analyst. I am one of very few medical psychoanalysts in the country who is a member of the psychoanalysis division of the American Psychological Association.

INTO THE FUTURE

Among recent theoretical developments, neurobiological formulations of psychoanalytic concepts deserve special mention, albeit with a proviso: descriptions of neurobiological mechanisms have not been capable of, and may never by capable of, supplanting psychological propositions. And, in fact, the most productive work in neurobiology involves work on the neuroanatomical structures and the neurophysiological processes that underlie psychoanalytic concepts. Rather than modifying its understanding of mental functioning on the basis of neurobiological findings, that is, psychoanalysis has pointed neurobiology in the direction of particularly promising conceptual and experimental endeavors. Thus we now have a body of literature that addresses topics of analytic concern: neurophysiological demonstrations of unconscious mental processes (Shevrin et al., 1992); neuroanatomical distinctions (e.g., between right brain and left brain) that correlated with Freud's notions of primary and secondary processes; research on the neurophysiological pathways of affective expression; and research on the impact of perceptual-environmental experiences on neurological development. Notions of "neuroplasticity" and of a "neural representational system" (Levin, 1991) have been proposed as bridge concepts linking neurobiological functioning to mental activity, including unconscious mental processes. In a recent book typifying this genre, Winson (1985) equates the Freudian unconscious with biogenetically ancient mechanisms that involve REM sleep and are located in the prefrontal cortex and its associated structures. Research that seeks to posit a neurobiological substrate for psychoanalytic concepts provides the same useful function as research into the psychological processes associated with neurobiological events.

All the foregoing testifies to the continuing vitality of psychoanalysis on the eve of the 21st century. Whereas the membership of the American Psychoanalytic Association, the oldest analytic organization in the United States, has remained stable over the past several years, the larger universe of psychoanalysis has been expanding, if one takes into account nonmedical organizations, such as the 4,000-member psychoanalysis division of the American Psychological Association.

It is true that the number of psychiatric residents entering analytic training has been declining. Of course, this correlates with a diminution of career interest in psychiatry across the board. That there is a continual flow of residents applying for training suggests that psychoanalytic and psychodynamic concepts retain their appeal. In 1991, the American Psychoanalytic Association established a Resident Fellowship Program to encourage and support psychiatric residents whose work to date evinces an understanding of the role of psychodynamic and psychoanalytic principles in clinical practice and research. Competition for Fellowships grows keener each year. In 1995, 15 Fellows were selected from a pool of 85 extraordinarily qualified applicants. From an international perspective, moreover, psychoanalysis is undergoing expansion rather than contraction. Membership in the International Psychoanalytical Association has grown as analysis has burgeoned in countries across the globe—Latin America, Germany, France, and elsewhere.

Psychoanalysis is a science committed to viewing conscious mental life with skepticism, to tracing causes to the past, to looking behind evasions, to searching for the truth embedded in the past, and to understanding human behavior as the outcome of dynamic conflict. Psychiatrists who have no interest in dreams, who never make slips of the tongue, and who are never puzzled by symptoms, inhibitions, or delusional thoughts will not be drawn to psychoanalytic explanation. Of course, many psychiatrists are intrigued by these experiences, which is why psychoanalysis continues to hold its own in the intellectual marketplace, along with other powerful explanatory systems that account for important aspects of human experience. In psychoanalytic inquiry, the risk of misunderstanding is great, the possibility of failure ever-present, and the promise of reward uncertain. What stands at the end, however, is the possibility of grasping more clearly the complexity of human experience. Psychiatrists drawn to this quest and animated by the profound clinical possibilities of the "talking cure" will continue to find psychoanalysis a most rewarding career.

REFERENCES AND RECOMMENDED READING

Brenner, C. (1982), *The Mind in Conflict*. New York: International Universities Press.

Blum, H. P., Kramer, Y., Richards, A. K., & Richards, A. R. (1989), *Fantasy, Myth, and Reality: Essays in Honor of Jacob A. Arlow*. New York: International Universities Press.

Gill, M. M. (1994), *Psychoanalysis in Transition: A Personal View*. Hillsdale, NJ: The Analytic Press.

Kohut, H. (1971), *The Analysis of the Self*. New York: International Universities Press.

Kohut, H. (1977), *The Restoration of the Self*. New York: International Universities Press.

Levin, F. (1991), *Mapping the Mind: The Intersection of Psychoanalysis and Neuroscience*. Hillsdale, NJ: The Analytic Press.

Reppen, J. ed. (1985), *Beyond Freud: A Study of Modern Psychoanalytic Theorists*. Hillsdale, NJ: The Analytic Press.

Richards, A. (1990), The future of psychoanalysis: The past, present, and future of psychoanalytic theory. *Psychoanal. Quart.* 59:347–369.

Richards, A. R. & Willick, M. S. (1986), *Psychoanalysis: The Science of Mental Conflict — Essays in Honor of Charles Brenner.* Hillsdale, NJ: The Analytic Press.

Shevrin, H., Williams, W. J., Marshall, R. E., et al. (1992) Event-related potential indicators of the dynamic unconscious. *Conscious. & Cog.,* 1:340–366.

Wallerstein, R. ed. (1992), *The Common Ground of Psychoanalysis.* Northvale, NJ: Aronson.

Winson, J. (1985), *Brain and Psyche: The Biology of the Unconscious.* New York: Random House.

⚹ 3 ⚹

Getting Rid of Rats

[PUBLIC PSYCHIATRY]

Carl C. Bell

Dr. Bell is President/CEO of the Community Mental Health Council, Inc., a private, not-for-profit, comprehensive mental health center on Chicago's southside. Dr. Bell is also a Clinical Professor of Psychiatry at the School of Medicine and of Public Health at the School of Public Health at the University of Illinois in Chicago. In addition, he is Co-Principal Investigator of the Chicago African-American Youth Health Behavior Project. He is a Fellow of the American Psychiatric Association, a member of the National Medical Association (past Chairman, Section on Psychiatry and Behavioral Science), a member of the Black Psychiatrists of America (past vice-president), a member of the American College of Psychiatrists, and a member of Alpha Omega Alpha. Dr. Bell is a Director of the National Commission on Correctional Health Care (Past Chairman), a former Director of the American Association of Community Psychiatrists, and an examiner for the American Board of Psychiatry and Neurology. Dr. Bell has coauthored one book, 14 chapters, and over 100 articles. He has been awarded the Dr. Martin Luther King, Jr., Fellowship of Cook County Physicians' Association and the E. Y. Williams Distinguished Senior Clinical Scholar Award by the Section on Psychiatry of the National Medical Association.

ACQUIRING A PUBLIC PSYCHIATRY ATTITUDE

Having gone to a predominately black medical school, Meharry Medical College in Nashville, Tennessee, I was professionally socialized to believe that public health principles should dictate a sane, ethical practice of medicine. Accordingly, if a patient came into my office with a rat bite and I cleaned the wound, gave the patient a tetanus shot, and gave the patient antibiotics along with a clean dressing, I would be a good physician. If, however, several patients from the same community came into my office with rat bites and all I did was sit in my office and treat rat bites, I would be a lousy physician because I did not go the extra step of working in the community to get rid of the rat. That is my understanding of public psychiatry. Part of the job involves getting rid of the various "rats" that plague the communities we serve.

We can exterminate these "vermin" directly or by the more effective method of soliciting help from many different people who don't like "rats" in their communities. The easiest "rats" to destroy are those that lend themselves to biotechnical interventions, such as the removal of lead paint to prevent lead encephalopathy. The more difficult "rodents" to get rid of are those which require psychosocial interventions, such as the prevention of drug abuse or violence. Since human behavior is overdetermined and results from many different influences, it is very difficult to demonstrate scientifically that psychosocial interventions actually make a difference. Yet most of us know that we are interpersonal creatures who are influenced by the physical, educational, social, psychological, emotional, and spiritual environments that surround us.

For the past 10 years I've been trying to get rid of the violence "rat," and I have been studying the effects of traumatic stress in an effort to treat the consequences of this type of "vermin," which chronically plagues the poor African-American community. In addition, I have sought to develop more primary and secondary prevention approaches to the problems of violence in the African-American community. In an endeavor to extend my influence and garner support for my ventures, I have published studies on the impact of violence on children and studies on violence prevention projects. Thus, in many ways, I feel my work provides a concrete example of some of the basic tenets of public psychiatry. My advice to medical students, residents, and young psychiatrists interested in a career in public psychiatry is to pay particular attention to public health philosophy while in training. Without this foundation, a public psychiatry profession won't be led by the proper principles that should be directing the course of the pursuit.

EARLY PUBLIC PSYCHIATRY VENTURES

Public psychiatry began with the mental hygiene movement in 1906, when Clifford Beers began to promote the idea that society had some role in a psychiatric patient's mental illness. Prior to his struggles, the origins of mental illness were thought to be innate, with the environment having little impact on their outcome. Shortly after the revelation that the environment had a role in mental illness, World War I occurred, and it became even more clear that people could be stressed by their environment and suffer psychiatric disorders. Despite this lesson, we soon forgot that environmental stressors could cause anxiety disorders. Freud reminded us of this when he began to write about neuroses, but unfortunately he attributed the cause of anxiety disorders to psychic causes rather than to the sexual assaults that were later found to have actually occurred in his "hysterical" patients.

Despite this misguided leadership, as a result of Freud's observations, child guidance clinics sprang up all over the country in a crusade to prevent parents from turning their children into psychiatric patients. The prevention that psychiatry promised was unrealistic, as it was believed that schizophrenia could be prevented by the development of proper parenting skills. After this bid at "rat" elimination, World War II occurred, and again we were reminded that stress in the environment could cause anxiety disorders. We saw massive public health initiatives in psychiatry as the military forces attempted to prevent the occurrence of psychiatric casualties of war by weeding out mentally unfit soldiers.

As Freud had predicted, after the war we quickly forgot the lessons of traumatic stress. Fortunately, the Group for the Advancement of Psychiatry was active in developing some postwar public policy on mental health issues in an endeavor to provide a measure of preventive psychiatry for the country. As there were many new biotechnical improvements that would prevent several categories of organic brain syndromes, these psychiatrists went after those "rats." In addition, while trying to provide mental health services for the public, they also attempted to establish mental health service infrastructures similar to those they had developed during their military experience. Physicians who are considering going into public psychiatry need to pay particular attention to the historical enterprises that were set in motion to ensure the public's mental health. This understanding will provide an excellent framework for what has been tried and worked versus what has failed, and will lay the groundwork to provide strategies for public psychiatry in the future.

In 1963, the Community Mental Health Centers Act mandated the establishment of comprehensive mental health centers designed to serve a catchment area with 200,000 residents. These centers were intended to provide five services (inpatient, psychiatric emergency services, day treatment, outpatient, and consultation and education) in a bid to provide primary, secondary, and tertiary prevention for the mentally ill in our country. It was during this era that I was in medical school and completed my psychiatric residency, and the idea of public psychiatry appealed to my sense of responsibility and duty. While in medical school, I completed several research projects and published a couple of empirically based articles on the public health status of the poor patients in North Nashville, Tennessee. These articles focused on some of the "rats" in the community at that time, for example, the nutritional status of the children and drug abuse habits of the adolescents in the area. So, early on, I learned the importance of contributing to the empirically based literature on poor and under-served populations, and I felt the thrill of exploring unexplored vistas in medicine.

NEEDED TRAINING AND EXPERIENCE

My residency training in psychiatry was extremely eclectic as I found myself surrounded by renowned analysts, psychopharmacologists, group therapists, family therapists, milieu therapists, day treatment specialists, emergency psychiatry specialists, child psychiatrists, inpatient psychiatrists, adolescent psychiatrists, forensic psychiatrists, neuropsychiatrists, neurologists, research psychiatrists, geriatric psychiatrists, administrative psychiatrists, academic psychiatrists, private practice psychiatrists, addiction specialists, general hospital psychiatrists, consultation-liaison psychiatrists, nurses, social workers, psychologists, art therapists, occupational therapists, medical records technicians, community representatives, and more. Since I was told that as a community psychiatrist my job would be to treat efficiently and effectively anyone who walked in the door, I assumed that I needed to learn at least the basic principles of all these "subspecialties" in order to be competent. This philosophy toward my training and subsequent practice of public psychiatry has taught me that the various "subspecialties" rarely talk to one another or read each other's literature; the result is a great loss of synergy and occasional turf wars about whose version of the truth is real. By attending to the basic principles involved in the various "subspecialties," a community psychiatrist can understand and function proficiently in many different domains. The bottom line is that budding public psychiatry residents and young psychiatrists need to be "jacks of all psychiatric trades" and "knowers of all principles" involved in all subspecialties in order to be good at their job.

On leaving my residency, and after two years in the Navy (where I screened thousands of recruits for fitness for duty and read thousands of MMPIs, thereby learning another public psychiatry lesson, that is, case finding), I embarked on a career in public psychiatry as a community psychiatrist. Clearly, this endeavor would allow me to function in a variety of roles as a psychiatrist, and, to be efficient and effective, I would have to develop an experiential base in many different aspects of psychiatry. I began with a focus on emergency room psychiatry in a general hospital in an underserved African-American community on Chicago's southside. I wrote several articles on how to treat patients who presented to the emergency room in order to prevent their hospitalization. Unfortunately, I was not sophisticated in the ways of the world, and I soon became frustrated with the shoddy way the general hospital administered its psychiatric services. When I began at the hospital as director of their psychiatric emergency service, I so greatly reduced admissions (which was the mandate I had been given by the hospital to fulfill their state contract) that the census of the hospital's psychiatric unit dropped precipitously. I later came to understand that the hospital also had a contrary mandate to keep their beds filled.

As a result, my labors were attacked as capricious, and I left after six months. As I look back, it is unfortunate that no one in management had the clear vision to tell me that I could have served both masters by reducing the admissions to the state hospital while keeping the general hospital psychiatric beds filled. The lesson I learned the hard way and want to pass on is that, to be effective in public psychiatry, you must understand and have leadership and management skills, which will help you to select competent people to work with and avoid taking on ambiguous roles or roles where there is responsibility with no authority.

At any rate, while I was at the hospital, in addition to sharpening my skills as an emergency room psychiatrist, I also had an opportunity to sharpen my skills as an inpatient psychiatrist and a consultation-liaison psychiatrist. I even developed a small private practice. There being a great need for psychiatric services in the poor, underserved neighborhood around the hospital, my tremendous caseloads provided a great deal of clinical experience in various areas of psychiatry. I also became involved in a forensic psychiatry case: One of my staff members had stabbed his girlfriend to death in the medical clinic next door, and I became an expert witness in his case. Later, I found myself sought out by various public defenders to give them expert witness opinions or testimony about various murder cases. They told me that, despite my not being a forensic psychiatrist, I had a way of keeping things plain and presented myself as a person who could explain the common sense of psychiatry.

PUBLIC PSYCHIATRY AS STAFF PSYCHIATRIST

A few months after I quit my job at the general hospital, I was able to find a part-time job as a staff psychiatrist at a city mental health outpatient clinic. Later, I landed a part-time position at the Chicago Board of Education. Fortunately, I had had a lot of good supervision by competent child psychiatrists, so, even though I was not a child psychiatrist, I felt comfortable in my role as a psychiatrist whose job it was to evaluate and triage the children being seen in one of the Chicago Board of Education's child evaluation centers. During this time I saw over 400 children and had the advantage of a complete battery of assessments (psychological, social service, teacher, school nurse, diagnostic educational, etc.) to help me make tentative diagnoses for the children I evaluated. Two years later I did a follow-up study on these youngsters to determine their outcome and learned, to my surprise, that many of my recommendations had been followed with some success.My stint at the city clinic allowed me to practice my diagnostic and outpatient medication management skills. I also took some time to delve deeper into the psyche of a few traumatized patients, only to see firsthand what Freud had described as repression and neurosis. Because I was concerned that there was a negative stereotype that poor, African-American patients didn't need psychoanalytic psychotherapy, I wrote about my experiences, which led to many interesting conversations with Merton Gill, a noted psychoanalyst. During my time in the community as a staff psychiatrist for the Department of Mental Health and Board of Education, I also had the opportunity to begin working part-time with a day treatment center that had hopes of becoming a comprehensive community mental health center (CMHC) in the future. Since a goal of mine in medical school was to return to Chicago and develop a comprehensive CMHC on Chicago's southside, I readily joined this initiative early in its development.

The lesson from this part of my professional life that I would like to pass on to psychiatrists considering going into public psychiatry is not to allow yourself to be placed in a leadership role before you have been able to develop a wide range of solid clinical skills. If you make this error, you will find yourself supervising clinicians on clinical issues who have more experience than you do, and it won't work out. When I finished my tour of duty in the Navy, I really had no business being a director of a psychiatric emergency department. I suppose the hospital gave me that title to appeal to my narcissism so as to attract me to the job. I really wasn't "directing" anything; I was an administrative clinician rather than a clinical administrator. The difference is that an administrative clinician doesn't have control over hiring or firing or over the budget. He or she mainly oversees the clinical operations. A clinical administrator is a clinician who has actual authority to determine the allocation of resources.

PUBLIC PSYCHIATRY IN A GENERAL HOSPITAL

After some administrative changes at the general hospital, I was offered an opportunity to return, and, having developed my clinical skills, I decided again to struggle with the leadership role that working in a general hospital psychiatric department would offer me. Initially things went really well, and as the "second banana," I basically ran the day-to-day clinical operations of the department while the chairman of the department (a truly kind, older gentleman) interfaced with the hospital. As the Associate Director of the Division of Behavioral and Psychodynamic Medicine, I was very clinically involved in the emergency room, the outpatient clinic, the inpatient psychiatric service, and the consultation-liaison service. I thus gained some experience in developing and writing clinical policies and procedures. I wasn't a clinical administrator, so I didn't have actual authority over resources; but I had made it a point to have charismatic and clinical authority and so had some indirect influence over resource allocation. My clinical opportunities allowed me to publish several articles on managing violence in the emergency room and on the misdiagnosis of black manic-depressive patients in the outpatient clinic. My administrative opportunities allowed me to develop my leadership skills and administrative clinician skills.

After about three years at this job, I again became frustrated with the manner in which the hospital managed its staff, and I resigned my leadership role although I stayed on at the hospital. I suspect that my political activity conflicted with the general hospital administration. I was very supportive of a community board's getting control of the funds that would establish the CMHC that began as the day treatment center I had worked in earlier. I believed that the hospital wanted control of those funds so they could exploit the community by using grants to cover the administrative costs that the hospital incurred—a common practice in many institutional/public partnerships. After the chairman of the division died and a patient of mine somehow jumped from a window on the fourth floor (likely owing to poor management, in that the hospital's psychiatric unit had several chiefs, one for nursing, one for psychiatry, one for social service, one for technicians, and so on, leaving the chief of the unit to be an administrative clinician rather than a real clinical administrator with budgetary and hire/fire control of staff), it became clear to me that I wasn't going to get the power I wanted to make the system work in an efficient and effective manner. Therefore, I left to go to work at the CMHC I had helped develop.

PUBLIC PSYCHIATRY IN A COMMUNITY MENTAL HEALTH CENTER

Since I hadn't gotten any support from the hospital in my "research" efforts, when I went to work at the CMHC as the medical director, I got a commitment for support to do research on issues that affected my psychiatric care of a predominately African-American population. Further, I made sure that I had a chief I could trust. As the medical director of a comprehensive CMHC, I had the opportunity to hone my skills in the areas of substance abuse, children, the chronically mentally ill, and geriatric and vocational rehabilitation populations, as well as with patients who needed residential and day treatment. I also took the opportunity to go out into the community again and get "rid of the rats." We began to do research on the needs of the African-American population and learned that victimization from various forms of violence was a major problem. I started to write about our work in the hope that other professionals would take up the challenge I had identified. I'm now told that I'm a national expert in this area (an expert being someone from out of town who has a suit and a briefcase and has written at least one article on the subject). We also investigated the phenomenon of isolated sleep paralysis in African-Americans and found this to be a fruitful area of investigation; our findings related this phenomenon to panic disorder.

After I had been medical director for several years (frequently an administrative clinician), the executive director (who was a clinical administrator) went on to bigger (not necessarily better) things, and a coworker and I drew straws to decide who would be the new CEO. Unfortunately, I lost, and, despite not really understanding how the business of the agency was run, I got the job. Fortunately, my coworker knew this and educated me on how the agency functioned. She managed the operation while I provided the leadership and functioned as a medical director/staff psychiatrist and part-time researcher. (I was lucky enough to get a talented social psychologist to work with me on many of our projects who kept the research respectable.) After several years of superb management, my coworker left the agency to care for her ailing grandmother. Fortunately, she had followed one of my rules for the best way to run an agency—to groom your replacement—and she left me with two highly competent people to do her job of managing the day-to-day operations. We began to train medical students and residents from several of the medical schools in Chicago and continued to improve on our research program. In addition, several of the staff got the academic bug and began to train students in the various disciplines that they represented at the agency.

The agency continues to do what academia proposes to do: service, research, and training. We also continue to be a model agency in our state and have been the front runners in a number of new initiatives in mental health in Illinois. A few years back, we decided that, since I was so busy trying to provide the leadership for the agency, functioning as a staff psychiatrist (we were able to hire an excellent medical director) and as a part-time researcher, it might be best to run the agency using a team concept. Accordingly, we formed the Executive Administrative Team, which managed the day-to-day operations of the agency and provided leadership as well. Because we thought we needed to get ready for "managed scare," we changed our titles, and I went from being Executive Director to President/CEO.

Since becoming the boss who is not a boss, I have learned about leadership, management, budgets, elevators, human resources, building maintenance, bank loans, contract and grant compliance, EEOC, management information systems, computers, OSHA requirements, accounting checks and balances, interfacing with a community board of directors, how to establish relationships with banks and vendors, how to influence people without their hating you too much, and how never to lose sight of the care of the staff and the patients they serve. In other words, I'm finally a real clinical administrator. I tell all new employees that how the agency treats them will determine how they treat their patients. We continue to break new ground in several areas of research, such as community studies of children exposed to violence and sleep disorders in African-Americans. And we continue to grow and evolve.

My quests for research, teaching, and publishing somehow got me on the faculties of various medical schools in Chicago, either as clinical faculty or lecturer, and I have found myself on the editorial boards of several journals. As I understood more clearly what public psychiatry consisted of, I was appointed to a consortium of national health organizations whose role it was to monitor and accredit the health care in our nation's jails, prisons, and juvenile detention centers. Thus, I was exposed to several other aspects of public psychiatry, those of correctional health care and the development of public policy. It soon became clear to me that the health of the nation is determined by the health care of the "least of us." Thus, for example, if we don't invest labor in identifying and treating incarcerated inmates who have tuberculosis, sooner or later they are going to be released into the general population and will infect my children. To keep this from happening, I have become involved with advocacy and public policy, which helps get "rid of the rat" not only in my surrounding catchment area, but in the country as a whole.

CONCLUSION

My efforts have been rewarded. I make a decent amount of money; I think I am respected by my colleagues; I am the boss at work who lets the employees run it; I have been one of the people on the cutting edge of issues that have changed the manner in which the country operationalizes its health care policies; and I have accomplished a goal I set for myself when I decided to go into psychiatry, which was to try to learn some of what was inside that black box we think of as the mind. After all, one of life's greatest adventures is exploring the unknown.

I have no idea where the future of public psychiatry is headed. I suspect that the future will mirror the past; that is, there won't be a major investment in providing very much for those who need the most. After all, this is America, so those who need the least will continue to get the most. But unless the basic values of the country change drastically, there will always be a need and some provision to ensure the public's mental health. There will always be some respectable work to be done in the area of public psychiatry. I think it is important to approach the work in public psychiatry as though you have possession of the ball at the 50-yard line of a one-mile football field. It is going to take a lot of work to get a touchdown, but, as long as you keep getting first downs and keep possession of the ball, the likelihood of burnout is drastically reduced because you will see gradual progress toward your goals.

RECOMMENDED READING

Acosta, F. X., Yamoto, J., & Evans, L. A. (1982), *Effective Psychotherapy for Low-Income and Minority Patients*. New York: Plenum Press.

Bell, C. C. (1994), Is psychoanalytic therapy relevant for public mental health programs? In: *Controversial Issues in Mental Health*, ed. S. A. Kirk & S. D. Einbinder. New York: Allen & Bacon, pp. 118–124.

Bell, C. C. (1993). The new community psychiatry–year 2000. *Hosp. Commun. Psychiat.*, 44:815.

Bell, C. C., Fayen, M., & Mattox, G. (1988), Training psychiatric residents to treat blacks. *J. Natl. Med. Assoc.*, 80:637–641.

Panzetta, A. F. (1985), Whatever happened to community mental health: Portents for corporate medicine. *Hosp. Commun. Psychiat.*, 36:1174–1179.

Talbott, J. A. (1979). Why psychiatrists leave the public sector. *Hosp. Commun Psychiat.*, 30:778–782.

❊ 4 ❊

HMO Psychiatry: Not All The Same

[HMO PRACTICE]

Richard J. Moldawsky

Dr. Moldawsky is a board-certified psychiatrist with the Southern California Permanente Medical Group (Kaiser Permanente) in Downey, California. After completing his psychiatric residency at Temple University Hospital in 1979, he was an inpatient unit director and Assistant Clinical Professor in the Department of Psychiatry and Human Behavior at the University of California, Irvine. While a member of the Department, he served as Assistant Director of the Psychiatric Consultation-Liaison Service. He held a joint faculty appointment with the Department of Medicine, for which he developed a core curriculum in psychiatric aspects of general medical practice for internal medicine residents training for primary care. Dr. Moldawsky has been with Kaiser Permanente for 12 years, six of which were spent as Chief of the Department of Psychiatry. In addition, he served as an elected member of the Executive Council of the Orange County Psychiatric Society, and, for three years, was President of the Orange County Chapter of Physicians for Social Responsibility. He has been active with California Health Decisions, a nonprofit community education organization, for the past 10 years.

As a medical student and psychiatric resident in the 1970s in Philadelphia, I was intrigued by the concept of the health maintenance organization (HMO), which, at the time, was primarily a California phenomenon. Kaiser Permanente, then as now, was the prototype organization. From 3,000 miles away, it appeared to offer socially responsible, nonelitist medical care in a comprehensive, organized system. It also seemed to relieve physicians of some of the headaches of private practice, such as billing and collecting fees, frequent night and weekend coverage, and competing for patients.

RESIDENCY

My psychiatric residency at Temple from 1976 to 1979 took place at a time when psychoanalysis was beginning to lose its central position in American psychiatry, although psychoanalysts and psychoanalytically oriented psychiatrists still held most of the prominent positions in university departments of psychiatry. The increasing role of psychopharmacology and the attention to utilization review and other cost-related issues were new phenomena. As residents we quickly learned that an admitting diagnosis of acute schizophrenic episode guaranteed you 14 days of care for the patient before you'd be asked to justify additional hospitalization.

Temple's faculty as a whole seemed to convey a curious blend of academic skepticism and therapeutic flexibility. Most of the faculty with whom I had regular contact were very clinically oriented and had what appeared to be a relative lack of interest for research. Psychodynamic therapy was still the gold standard; there was little discussion of brief psychotherapy as a specific modality of treatment. However, most supervisors understood that patients with limited funds or no insurance could benefit from some form of short-term therapy. A few psychoanalysts did have a surprisingly short-term orientation. There was no discussion about HMOs as a practice option, but it was always in the back of my mind as I tried to imagine how I wanted to spend my professional life.

These diverse and somewhat iconoclastic influences prepared me well for some of the changes brewing in American psychiatry. The biopsychosocial model had begun to take hold, and the "eclectic" psychiatrist had become the new ideal. One needed to have diagnostic competence, because differential therapeutics now meant something, since not all patients were to receive psychoanalysis or chlorpromazine any more. One also needed to modify and integrate concepts of nonpsychoanalytic psychotherapies, using systems, cognitive, and behavioral perspectives, all of which reflected not only their own intellectual bases, but also trends in American culture. The almost complete lack of objective data as to what really "worked" in psychiatric treatment seemed to provide a license to embrace or reject any approach, or to make up your own and call it your personal brand of eclecticism.

TAKING THE PLUNGE

As I neared the end of my residency, I was certain only that it was time to leave Philadelphia after 12 years and that I didn't know what I wanted for a real job. I had always enjoyed the intellectual stimulation of academia, although I realized that Temple wasn't the typical academic setting. It seemed that a different university setting would (as I'd tell anyone) "keep my options open," help me pass the boards, and protect me from making a real professional commitment. I believed that once you left academia, it would be be almost impossible to reenter it, since there would be little opportunity for research or publishing "on the outside." I did interview for several university positions in Philadelphia, Virginia, and California, and I also interviewed with Kaiser in southern California; one of my fellow residents had begun there six months earlier and liked it so far. But I wasn't ready to make what seemed to me to be a long-term commitment, so I opted for a junior faculty, ward-chief position at the University of California, Irvine (UCI). My wife and I took the plunge so that we could experience California and I could sample a new kind of professional existence.

UCI was a more typical academic department, with several prominent faculty members writing and talking about their interests in what seemed to be a receptive atmosphere. When I found out that there were weekly meetings of the university hospital-based faculty (including myself), I anticipated lively, stimulating discussions. I was dumbfounded when it became clear that these meetings were almost exclusively focused on financial matters: relationships between the university and Orange County's mental health department, utilization review, Medi-Cal (Medicaid in California), and the university's share of faculty private practice earnings. As a ward attending, part of my daily job was to write a progress note (of any length or quality) on all patients, in addition to resident and medical student notes, so that the hospital could bill the state or private insurer. I was learning quickly that the business side of medical practice was a force that could not be avoided.

While at UCI, I made some attempts to cultivate a private practice. Most of my patients started as inpatients on my ward who had private insurance or could afford my $60 fee: I took some Medi-Cal patients too; the state would pay $36 at the time for a one-hour visit. Our daughter was born in July 1980, and the combination of my wanting to be an active and present father, the absence of nearby family, and my general lack of skill at marketing myself kept my limited practice limited. As united as my wife and I were in our wish to move away from the east, we found that first year or two were very difficult. At least I had the structure of a job, and I took our only car to work each day, which is a recipe for major strain in California.

I was well thought of at UCI, though some wondered why I didn't involve myself in some kind of research. Having minimal exposure to formal research at Temple, no skills (or interest) in grant writing, and no burning questions I felt compelled to explore scientifically, I began to realize that my interest in the academic life was quite limited. As much as I enjoyed (and still enjoy) trying to stay current with the literature, the more rigorous (and, to me, tediously methodical) aspects of research did not entice me. I was asked by a senior, respected colleague, Louis A. Gottschalk, to coauthor a book chapter he'd been asked to write, a task I was truly honored to take on, and I did so with relish. The topic was adverse reactions and toxicity of anxiolytic drugs, essentially a large literature review. I did most of the legwork and the actual writing and found the experience very satisfying. For a self-styled academic dilettante, I was enormously pleased to see my name in the table of contents with people who were "stars" in the psychiatric firmament at the time.

In 1982, the university appointed William E. Bunney, Jr. as Chair of the Department of Psychiatry and Human Behavior. An important figure in biological research at NIMH for many years, he wanted to create a major research center at UCI. I could see myself only in a peripheral role in such a place, and, although I was respected for my clinical and teaching skills, I decided I needed to move from "keeping my options open" to actually selecting one! No one at UCI ever had implied to me that I should leave or look elsewhere, but I knew I didn't want to be a ward chief forever. I still wasn't any more aggressive or proficient at building up a private practice, and neither my wife nor I could get excited about the evening and weekend hours that such a career would likely entail.

THE HMO EXPERIENCE

Having maintained close ties with my fellow Temple resident who had now been with Kaiser for about four years, I decided once again to look into HMO practice, encouraged by the apparent long-term stability of such a career, his generally positive experience, the lack of other opportunities in the area, and our family's desire to stay put geographically. In May 1983, I accepted a position with the Southern California Permanente Medical Group, the large medical partnership that contracts with the Kaiser Foundation Health Plan, a large insurance company, to provide medical care for its members. These two entities, in combination with Kaiser Foundation Hospitals, constitute Kaiser Permanente in southern California. There isn't, surprisingly enough, a unitary structure called Kaiser Permanente. The Southern California Region, as it's known in Kaiserspeak, serves over two million people from Bakersfield to San Diego, organized into ten service areas.

My primary job, in the Bellflower Service Area just south of Los Angeles, was to be the primary consultation psychiatrist for the general hospital, covering the emergency room and inpatient units and also being available to nonpsychiatric physicians in the clinics. It was assumed that this would take about half of my time. The other half was to be spent seeing my own outpatients in the psychiatry department. I had no inpatient psychiatric responsibility, a major change from my UCI experience. The consultation component was something I had always enjoyed, both as a resident and at UCI. It allowed me to learn the ropes of this massive system, to meet many Kaiser physicians and other staff, and to get them to know me and my abilities, a valuable political tactic. After two years, I would be eligible for partnership, and physician voting would be based in large part on their direct knowledge of me.

It was clear from the outset that my immediate accessibility and ability to make quick decisions and dispositions of patients "in the house" were of highest value to my consultees, and their interest in the finer points of effective consultation, such as whether they told patients I was coming to see them and why, could be meaningfully introduced only if the physician felt I was addressing his or her needs for rapid assistance. Some were actually quite interested in aspects of diagnosis and psychopharmacology, and it was gratifying to be able to expound as an expert. Many held to the "I-can't-find-an-organic cause-so-it-MUST-be-psychiatric" mindset, and challenging this notion was among the most thorny of problems.

In my first job in a nonacademic setting, I did not deal with medical students, residents, fellows or other trainees. Attending physicians dealt directly with other attendings and consultants, and the emphasis was on clinical care; whether a case was interesting or had teaching or research value was secondary. Those who have spent most or all of their professional lives in university settings have a tendency to look askance at "local medical doctors," but I was impressed by their knowledge and commitment to patient care.

My outpatient work began easily, with a steady stream of clinical problems covering virtually every diagnostic category and treatment modality. Although I might hospitalize some patients in our free-standing psychiatric hospital, where they can be treated by other Kaiser staff before returning to me, most of my patients are treated solely by me. I am responsible for seeing a certain number of new patients each week, but, depending on my ability to manage my time and caseload, my ongoing patients can be seen as frequently as necessary. Some patients see a psychiatric social worker or clinical psychologist as a "primary therapist" and see me only for medication, a collaboration that usually goes smoothly, as we all work in the same physical site.

A little more than half of our patients are self-referred, and the rest are referred by other physicians. Our organization does not mandate that a primary care physician be a "gatekeeper," although some departments have chosen to function in a referral-only manner. This is one of many examples of how HMOs and managed care organizations vary. I have made it one of my crusades to correct some of these misconceptions wherever I can, because I believe that much of the anti-HMO, anti-managed care sentiment in our profession and within society in general is based on beliefs that are simply untrue of a good deal of HMO and managed care practice.

Major Themes

In my experience treating psychiatric outpatients at Kaiser, several major themes have been consistently important, and I doubt that these themes are significantly different elsewhere. The emphasis is on making a rapid and accurate diagnostic evaluation. Treatment recommendations should incorporate the patient's perceptions, not only of what he or she thinks is the problem, but also what he or she can or will accept as treatment. I have found that understanding why the patient has come *now*, as opposed to, say, last week or next month, to be the most useful bridge to establishing a therapeutic alliance of any kind, even (or especially) if the patient is here only to get a disability form signed. Lazare, Eisenthal, and Wasserman's (1975) article, "A Customer Approach to Patienthood," has been very helpful in categorizing the patient's needs. If these needs are not identified and addressed explicitly in some way, little progress is possible. This lesson was hammered home to me repeatedly as a first-year resident by Dr. Roy Stern, my first supervisor at Temple, well before I encountered Lazare.

Most patients don't want or expect long-term therapy, and despite the prevalence of chronic mental illnesses and personality disorders, my patients think in terms of problems adjusting to stressors at home, at work, to medical illnesses, and the like. They look for help in getting "back on track" rather than definitively resolving intrapsychic conflicts. Expecting mostly episodic care, they seek help when they feel ill in some way, and to continue coming when they feel better usually seems silly to them.

My psychotherapy patients are usually seen every week or two for between four and eight sesssions, especially when there is no medication involved. In some cases, I will formally spell out the "dosage" and frequency of these sessions, in the manner of James Mann's (1973; Mann and Goldman, 1981) time-limited psychotherapy, although with others, I'll take the "let's-meet-a-few-times-and-reevaluate" approach. Patients who seem fearful of the process are often reassured by not feeling coerced into a longer commitment to therapy. Psychiatrists who recommend psychotherapy usually need to explain more about how talking helps. Some patients are quite surprised when I offer to be their psychotherapist; they expect me to prescribe medications and refer them to a "counselor" for therapy.

Although over the course of many years patients or their family members will change or lose jobs and therefore, at times, their Kaiser insurance, many patients stay with us for most of their lives. From the standpoint of the psychiatrist, then, one has the opportunity to follow these people over the long term, which facilitates the episodic, intermittent treatment at which we excel. It is remarkable and satisfying when a patient, having seen me only briefly, calls me after two, five, or eight years and recalls enough about the experience to want to see me again. Recently, I saw a patient who showed me that she still keeps in her wallet my business card, which I gave her in 1985 – transitional object to be sure, but it also speaks to the stability of such an established treatment setting.

Owing to its sheer size, patients have multiple experiences with Kaiser personnel, from the receptionist at the emergency room to the primary physician, from the billing clerk to the pharmacist. These experiences lead to a kind of "institutional transference," which can work for or against you. One learns to be sensitive to this issue. Even though it's not exactly the usual therapeutic material, if a patient's previous view of the organization is slanted one way or the other, you are well advised to be prepared to hear about how long it took to get this appointment, how no one explained about the copayment, and so on. Defusing such (often totally valid) concerns usually needs to occur before much else can be accomplished. The other side of the coin is that, as physicians and psychiatrists, we are vulnerable to developing a problematic "institutional countertransference," in which the large organization becomes our explanation/apology/excuse when things go wrong. There are some limitations to the amount and kinds of care we can provide, but, in general, as long as these parameters are identified and addressed early in the doctor–patient relationship, these realities can be seen more as challenges than barriers. It's better to ask "What can we do given what's available?" than to focus on what we could do if only Kaiser would let me see the patient twice a week, or pay me for a home visit, or waive a high copayment.

Given the ambiguously worded benefit language and the considerable freedom to manage patient care as one sees fit, I can advocate strongly for my patients with good results. If a patient might benefit from a newer, expensive antidepressant, I prescribe it. I have never been told to stop seeing a patient because he or she has been in treatment "too long" or isn't "getting better." And a neurologist or internist isn't required to approve my sending a patient for a CT or MRI scan, or for any other work-up I think is indicated. Every time I read or hear about managed care horror stories in which endless approval mechanisms delay care, I think I must be leading a charmed existence.

None of this should be taken to mean that Kaiser isn't attentive to costs, limited resources, patient demands, demands of purchasers of our health plan (mostly employers), and all the factors that drive the health care reform debate. However, physicians in general, and perhaps ours more so because we have enjoyed a certain insulation from some of these external pressures, are particularly resentful of being told what to do. We've all been trained to think exclusively of the individual physician–patient relationship. The recent shift to considering ourselves as a large group of "providers" caring for a "population" of two million people means that deciding what's best in terms of staffing, prescription benefits, kinds of hospital beds, and other ponderous questions feels foreign and, in a sense, unethical and unprofessional to many individual physicians, who prefer to think of those issues as someone else's problem (until, of course, it affects their practice or pocketbook).

ADMINISTRATION

I have had the opportunity as part of my Kaiser experience to grapple with some of these issues not only as a clinician but also as an administrator. In August 1985, I was appointed to head this department of 11 psychiatrists, 5 clinical psychologists, and 25 or so psychiatric social workers, along with our clerical staff. As chief, I still spent about 80% of my time seeing patients, consistent with the organization's propensity for keeping administrative costs low. Just as important, my credibility with my fellow psychiatrists seemed related to whether I was perceived as dealing with the same day-to-day clinical problems they faced. At the time of my appointment, I felt it was necessary to be based at the clinic all day, so I relinquished my consultation hat.

In our medical group, a department chief's actual job is minimally defined, and one can usually structure the role in a variety of ways. For me, the experience opened my eyes to how psychiatry is viewed throughout our large organization, by administrators, other physicians and providers. In comparison with the major worries of higher level decision makers, issues relating to the role and practice of psychiatry were rarely on the front burner. Although it was frustrating that these people didn't seem to have sufficient appreciation and sophistication about the role of psychological factors and psychiatric illnesses in general medical care, this "benign neglect" allowed me, in my own way, to introduce to my own staff larger issues, such as how we address employers' needs, and to address many operational problems. As an example of the latter, we had no formal mechanism by which nonphysician therapists could have their patients see a psychiatrist for a medication evaluation. The existing "system" led to a highly uneven distribution of the workload. In the early days of the department, such informality was adaptive, but as we grew larger, more of these kinds of organizational issues called for written agreements. Most of my psychiatrist colleagues were more tuned in to the details of daily life in the clinic, and there was relatively little interest or enthusiasm for the larger issues facing Kaiser in general. My role as their "ambassador" to the rest of the organization seemed to be valued insofar as I could shield them from some of these external pressures. I didn't particularly think that I could, or should, shield them from those problems, and this, at times, led to my being seen as traveling in a somewhat different orbit from theirs and less attentive to their needs. That cost me some of their support.

On a day-to-day basis, though, I very much enjoyed the mix of clinical and administrative work. When my action could resolve a staff–patient or staff–staff conflict, it was very satisfying. Clinical rewards tend to come more gradually, however. What was more painstaking, but just as important, was being a spokesperson, not just for my department, but almost for psychiatry as a profession, in dealing with (the much, much larger) nonpsychiatric components of the organization. Outside my own department, I was, deservedly or not, the expert on all matters psychologic, and virtually all questions of "stress," "psychosomatics," "burnout," or other vaguely emotion-related issues were routed to me for my learned input.

I decided not to undertake a second six-year term as chief, primarily on the basis of feedback indicating that I didn't have sufficient support of my psychiatrist colleagues to continue in that role. While a painful blow, it has allowed me to concentrate more fully on clinical issues, to remain active in the organization in other ways, and assume a curious elder-statesman role in the department. I have been cochair of the hospital's ethics committee and have been active in developing clinical guidelines for the treatment of depression by primary care physicians, two activities that not only have been interesting in their own right, but also have helped me maintain diverse professional activities.

I've made a few small contributions to the psychiatric literature, almost entirely for my own interest and amusement. While some of the writing has been related to my HMO experience, it's definitely a sideline activity, done on my own time. We do have the capacity and support to do clinical research, but that's not my cup of tea. In this nonacademic setting, I can be a bit of the academician without worrying where my grant is coming from.

After 12 years in HMO practice with Kaiser, I have probably seen the best and worst of this kind of psychiatry, and I don't think such a setting is either a guarantee of good care or a setup for bad treatment. In our setting, there is little external pressure to do *excellent* work. One can relatively easily do an adequate job, which is often seen in quantitative terms alone. Admittedly, quality is very hard to measure, even though we tend to think we know it when we see it.

As I noted earlier in commenting on my consultation experience, rapidity of response and disposition tend to be rewarded in the outpatient clinic as well. This seems linked, in part, to the concept of Kaiser member as customer/consumer, with us as vendor/provider. To provide high quality clinical care sometimes means doing the right thing for the patient but the "wrong" thing for the customer. The patient might need a push to return to work, but the customer didn't get the disability he or she came for. The most appropriate treatment for the patient might be psychotherapy, but the customer wants Prozac. A substance abuser insists that depression's the problem. The ability to "negotiate" a treatment plan with the patient is an important skill, so that the patient feels that his or her needs are being addressed and that you don't feel railroaded into providing a service you feel is clinically out of line.

In our HMO, there is no shortage of clinical work, even though the organization is actively pursuing new members and trying to keep current ones enrolled. Although I don't have to recruit patients personally, I can't let myself believe that the patient will simply have to be satisfied with whatever I have to offer. I can't let phone messages go unanswered or prescriptions go unfilled. An individual patient's dissatisfaction with me or a decision to switch to a different psychiatrist isn't money out of my pocket. Although this is one of the core distinctions of this kind of HMO practice, it's a mindset that can lead to poor and disrespectful care. Whereas psychiatrists have had some training in the importance and meaning of money changing hands, most of our patients think they've already paid us for our service; and, in a very real sense, they have paid us with their monthly premiums. On the other hand, from the psychiatrist's point of view, if someone specifically insists on seeing only me because of something he or she has heard about me, the only actual reward is the compliment itself (and, to me, it's a big one). I don't earn more than my colleagues because of it.

Primary responsibility for staying current with professional knowledge is yours. Although academic roundsmanship is frowned upon, it's important to rely on more than just drug detail people to keep up. Being part of Kaiser is being part of a 50-year tradition of medical care that, after all, has been quite a success story. Despite the pitfalls of being part of such a large organization, you want to be a part of trying to do things better; and, if you're not something of a self-starter, you'll begin to think that absolutely everyone you see is depressed and needs Prozac. Certainly this will be true for some, but you'll do well to have skill and comfort with some form of brief dynamic psychotherapy, cognitive therapy, behavior therapy, and couples work, in addition to your medication arsenal. As the aphorism has it, if all you've got is a hammer, everything looks like a nail; it makes for sloppy psychiatry.

CONCLUSION

Readers should generalize from my experience with Kaiser to other HMO practices with great caution. The idea that all HMOs are essentially the same is simply inaccurate. Similarly, all managed care is not the same. Those considering psychiatry in a managed care or HMO setting need to look at each setting as a separate organism. I couldn't tell you if a Kaiser psychiatrist's practice in North Carolina, Oregon, or Ohio is like mine, except to say that his or her treatment approach is also based on a short-term orientation. If you're exploring different options, make no assumptions about how things are done in any particular place.

A committed, competent psychiatrist can deliver quality care almost anywhere. It's important to think about your own personal and professional values. What kind of lifestyle are you looking for? How much money do you want/need? What kind of professional gratification do you crave? Are you a solitary sort or a more gregarious type? What about working with nonmedical therapists and nonpsychiatric physicians? What about the demands of family or community? To what degree do you see psychiatry as a job or a profession?

When a patient gets discouraged when he or she doesn't get better with or can't tolerate a particular medication, I usually say that it's a matter of "fit" between patient and drug, not that there's something specifically wrong with the patient or the drug itself. HMO practice, and presumably other types of practice, are also a matter of "fit." A good fit is very satisfying, and even the side effects are easily tolerated.

REFERENCES AND RECOMMENDED READING

Bennett, M. J. & Wisneski, M.J. (1979), Continuous psychotherapy within an HMO. *Amer. J. Psychiat.*, 136: 1283–1287.

Hoyt, M. F. & Austad, C. S. (1992), Psychotherapy in a staff model health maintenance organization: Providing and assuring quality care in the future. *Psychotherapy*, 29:119–129.

Lazare, A., Eisenthal, S., & Wasserman, L. (1975), The customer approach to patienthood. *Arch. Gen. Psychiat.*, 32:553–558.

Mann, J. (1973), *Time-Limited Psychotherapy*. Cambridge, MA: Harvard University Press.

Mann, J. & Goldman, R. (1981), *A Casebook in Time-Limited Psychotherapy*. New York: McGraw-Hill.

Schneider-Braus, K. (1987), A practical guide to HMO psychiatry. *Hosp. Commun. Psychiat.*, 38:876–879.

Schreter, R. K., Sharfstein, S. S., & Schreter, C. A., eds. (1994), *Allies and Adversaries: The Impact of Managed Care on Mental Health Services*. Washington, DC: American Psychiatric Press.

❋ 5 ❋

Managing Care

[MANAGED CARE]

Michael J. Bennett

Dr. Bennett is Corporate Vice President for Medical Services for Merit Behavioral Care Corporation, the country's largest behavioral healthcare management company. He is also Clinical Associate Professor of Psychiatry at Harvard Medical School. In addition to his many corporate functions, Dr. Bennett continues to see patients privately and is actively engaged in teaching and supervision. He lectures and presents interactive workshops nationally and internationally and has written extensively about focal psychotherapy and managed behavioral healthcare. One of the original staff of the Harvard Community Health Plan (HCHP), which was the first organization to provide mental health services to an enrolled population as a basic benefit, Dr. Bennett oversaw the development of that HMO's mental health program. On his departure from HCHP after 22 years, an award was created in his name, to be given annually to a member of that organization for contributions to mental health managed care.

BEGINNINGS

In 1943, when I was in the second grade at P. S. 180 in Brooklyn, I was selected for my first managerial role: milk monitor. In retrospect, I learned all I needed to know about management and about managed care from that experience: supply what people need to function effectively, do it in a timely fashion, and distribute it equitably and you will succeed.

Raised in the waning days of WWII in the borough of Brooklyn, I am a first-generation Jewish-American only child of mixed eastern European ancestry, the first in my extended family to attend college and the first to "make it" into the professional world. The study of philosophy and European literature in college came naturally, and science did not, but there were strong cultural and family imperatives toward a career in medicine, law or business. Since I am an ACOA (the adult child of an accountant), the resultant ambivalence about numbers ruled out the third possibility, leaving only the first two as ego-syntonic ambitions. An influential primary care physician, who visited often, was a model, but my interest in things psychological was dominant from an early age. That interest was consolidated during my third year of college, when a paper on Dostoevski's (1943) *Notes From the Underground* brought me accolades from an admired professor and his advice that I "consider becoming a psychologist." I did, and decided to become a psychiatrist instead.

TRAINING

Following medical school, which proved to me that my future lay in practice, I accepted a residency at Massachusetts Mental Health Center (MMHC), a bastion of psychoanalytic thinking and teaching at the time. Although I took to dynamic psychiatry naturally, my mentor was not the charismatic Elvin Semrad, but rather Jack Ewalt, who was a straight-talking Texan with a clarity and conciseness of thinking and an emphasis on getting things done that offered a refreshing counterbalance to the dominant emphasis on "hovering neutrality." I found the pace and passive posture of exploratory psychotherapy frustrating but appreciated the opportunity it afforded to learn about my patients in depth. I also found that I missed medicine.

My romance with medicine was rekindled in my third year of residency, when I opted to create a bridge between MMHC and the nearby Beth Israel Hospital, an institution known for a strong relationship between the departments of medicine and psychiatry and therefore a perfect place to learn liaison psychiatry. Under Grete Bibring, psychiatrists such as Norman Zinberg, Ralph Kahana, and Arthur Kravitz practiced at the medical–psychological interface, which reminded me that psychiatry was a medical specialty. As a result of my interest and enthusiasim, I was asked to perform all the consults for the male medical service and found myself spending 20 hours rather than the planned three hours per week at the Beth Israel. Although they were also psychoanalysts, my teachers placed emphasis on character assessment, rapid formulation, and focused, brief interventions. At the same time, at Mass Mental Health Center, I was attempting to help schizophrenic patients largely through psychotherapy, since in those days there was little encouragement to use medication except in the most acute phase of the illness. The balance in my training was wonderful!

My interest in managed care sprang from experiences in liaison psychiatry, reinforced by an unanticipated return to management. As a member of the Berry Plan, through which military service was deferred while I completed my residency, I joined the Army and was stationed on Okinawa. After a brief stint running a dispensary, I became de facto chief of psychiatry at a 500-bed hospital after the only other psychiatrist on the island rotated home, and I was left alone to manage a population slightly in excess of 100,000. My hospital chief, a Mississippian Colonel named Cox, in response to my concern about how I could manage the assignment, gave me a piece of advice I carry with me still: "Mahhk," he said, "Jus' put out de fahs!" Within a week I had designated all the social work technicians as psychotherapists, all the dispensary doctors as gatekeepers, and all the corpsmen as psychiatric physician assistants. My career in management was launched.

HMO PSYCHIATRY

Prior to leaving for Okinawa, I had asked two admired supervisors, Jack Vorenberg, the acting Chief of Psychiatry at the Beth Israel, and Arthur Kravitz, my old liaison supervisor, to watch for job opportunities for me. On my return, the former found me a job working with Tom Dwyer, a psychiatrist who had acquired a grant to teach medical psychology to house officers at Massachusetts General Hospital; the latter placed me in contact with the planners for the Harvard Community Health Plan, which was on the drawing board and scheduled to open sometime in 1969. Art correctly assumed that I would share his opinion that the health maintenance organization concept, new at that time in New England, was the logical extension of liaison psychiatry. A job was open, and I took it. I also took every other job in sight and by mid-1968 was working halftime as a supervisor at Mass Mental Health Center, halftime at Mass General, a few hours per week consulting and seeing patients at the Concord Reformatory, and a few hours at the Beth Israel, teaching liaison techniques to medical students. At the same time, I began a private practice.

When Harvard Community Health Plan opened its doors in October 1969, I was on its staff—one of two psychiatrists. My partner left, replicating my army experience and leaving me as de facto chief. At 33, I found myself working hand in hand with Dick Nesson, the visionary medical director who became one of my most influential mentors, to develop mental health services for a diverse population. Drawing on my liaison experience, I attempted to exploit the concept of primary care, central to the plan's philosophy, and to develop a model of indirect service. Emulating one of my heroes, Michael Balint, a British psychoanalyst who spent much of his career teaching British surgeons to do psychotherapy, I ran "Balint groups" for internists, nurses, surgeons, pediatricians, and others. I hired psychiatric nurses, and we began a variety of programs to support a mental health role for doctors and nurses while keeping our direct services limited to evaluation, consultation, and brief psychotherapy. The strategy failed. In specialist-rich Boston and with a sophisticated population of members, a diversity of direct services was demanded and required. Reluctantly, over the early years I found myself with a growing panel of patients, head of a burgeoning department. I also found myself returning to teaching, my early and persistent love, and I began to write about my experiences in prepaid group practice as a distinct emerging clinical model, a culture, springing from the context of prepayment. The department flourished, with a spirit of experimentation, shared excitement, and constant learning.

Two factors shaped my approach to the clinical work. First was the recognition that I was no longer serving only my individual patients but, as a manager and as a clinician, was now responsible for the care of a population. This was sharply at variance with my training, which emphasized the relationship with individual patients. Second, with the passage of state legislation in 1976, making it necessary to begin serving patients with chronic conditions, who had previously been excluded from coverage, it became clear that the models of brief psychotherapy I had learned and practiced (as taught by such theoreticians as David Malan, Peter Sifneos, and James Mann) were not adequate as a general strategy to meet the needs of a diverse population. Having hired predominantly traditionally trained clinicians like myself, I found the staff challenged, as I was, to reconcile conventional notions of health and illness with the rapid pace and heavy demands of a population that was seeking service at an alarming rate. We drew on the emerging adult developmental literature and on our own observations that patients sought help intermittently and that they healed discontinuously rather than continuously, often asking us for less than we had been trained to provide. Gradually, a model of "primary mental health care" began to evolve, not unlike what I had learned as a liaison psychiatrist: intermittent contact with the (mental) health care system at times of need, with ready access, targeted interventions, and high expectations of our patients for self-care in between. We also began to develop maintenance groups to address some of the psychosocial needs of the chronically and persistently ill but relied heavily on medication in caring for this part of the population.

In 1980, I decided to leave management. My reasons were varied but had to do mainly with changes in the organization, which had entered a conservative phase. I had found the systems development exciting but had little interest in the emerging emphasis on work expectations, productivity, and efficiency. I wished to write, to continue to treat patients, and to do more teaching. In retrospect, I was getting ready to leave, though it took me 11 more years actually to do so. Increasingly, my attention was drawn to new learning. I became a comanager of the chronic care program and began to develop my skills in psychopharmacology. In the mid-1980s, I began to look for new opportunities. In preparation, I decided that psychiatric boards, long deferred, were now an imperative. I studied for a year and was amazed at my still existing capacity to learn and to do well in an exam. Somehow the head hunters learned that I might be available and considering a change (though I never contacted a job broker). I interviewed for two senior managerial jobs and was surprised when I was offered both–shocked, actually, since I was "fishing" and not really ready for a move. Like my patients, I was to find that readiness cannot be forced; when it occurs, however, it insists on being recognized. My readiness was to come to my attention in an unusual way.

TRANSITION

In 1990, as part of a new program, I was offered a three-month sabbatical. My wife and I had no difficulty in deciding how to spend our time. With our youngest daughter in camp, we elected to spend six weeks camping in Norway, which we had each visited early in our lives and longed to see again. I did not feel, however, that the plan was complete, since I was seeking a renewal. I felt stuck, needing to make a change, but unaware of what I wanted or needed. Psychotherapy was out. I had had a personal analysis, had treated many patients myself, and had little sense that I would find anything new through conventional therapy. Instead, I arranged for us to spend a week in a workshop run annually on a farm in Norway by the director of the Boston Psychodrama Institute, who is a Norwegian.

The experience was compelling and transforming. As the only Americans and the only couple totally unfamiliar with psychodrama and bioenergetics, the two techniques used, we were completely out of our familiar element. For my wife, who is a nurse practitioner and who has been a senior manager, as well as for me, it was a rare experience of being a follower rather than a leader. For the first time in my life, I felt totally part of a group and totally a participant. The workshop was conducted partly in Norwegian (with translators) and partly, in deference to us, in English. The experience was intense: we laughed, cried, fought, learned, lived together for a week, immersed in our own and each other's dramas. When my time came to be the subject of a psychodrama, I found myself symbolically killing and burying my job to the resounding support of a Greek chorus of my new friends. It was inescapable proof to me that my only reason for not making a change was that I was afraid to do so.

The fear of change was not surprising. In 1990 I was 54 years old, with one ten-year-old child and two older daughters, both in college. I had a secure position, had accumulated six months of sick time, was paid well, and had excellent fringe benefits. My work was familiar and

I was good at it. I had the respect of colleagues, many of whom I had hired and who were my friends. Weighing against these factors was my sense of tedium and a wish to do something new. My wife and children had encouraged me to take the risk.

My opportunity came shortly after I returned to Boston, when I learned that American Biodyne, a privately owned behavioral health care company, had acquired a contract to manage mental health and substance abuse services for Blue Cross and Blue Shield of Massachusetts. I had known Biodyne's founder and CEO, Nick Cummings, for some years and believed I could work with him. I phoned and asked if he needed a medical director. The courtship began, and three months later the job was offered and I accepted. Since I had been a strong advocate of integrated mental health services for many years, I had to come to terms with the concept of the carve-out: mental health and substance abuse services financed, provided, and managed apart from general medical care. How did this work? What of the relationship with medicine and, my old love, indirect service and liaison? I came to see that the structure had distinct advantages and addressed many of the problems that had bothered me in my latter years at HCHP: centralized services with no link with employers; little outreach into the community or connection with community resources; funding that had to be reconciled with medical and surgical budgets that were often viewed as more compelling than mental health budgetary needs; and, most important, an insular approach that shied from confronting the needs of the broader community or the obvious challenge to reform the system at large. These features appeared to more than compensate for the loss of easy rapport with the other parts of the medical care system.

The transition involved other important matters as well. I had defined myself as a clinician and was reponsible in 1990 for approximately 200 patients. The new role would not be clinical. Biodyne was controversial, an organization developed by psychologists which was now becoming mainstream; my colleagues would be critical. Of course, this was nothing new. I had been arguing with my psychiatric colleagues for many years about such issues as allocation of clinical resources, the need for clinical efficiency through focused interventions, and the problems associated with overtreatment. At my tenth medical school reunion, I had found myself characterized as the class socialist, since HMOs at that time were considered a harbinger of socialized medicine. Now I was to become a capitalist, though with the same convictions. The question remained, how would I feel about myself if I gave up practicing? Did I have to reinvent myself?

I terminated with most of my patients, keeping only those who wished to follow me and who could be effectively treated with the irregular schedule I would now have, and began my new job in March of 1991. My time initially was involved with managing utilization, which required drawing on my relationships in the professional community, working with clinicians and institutions to develop alternative levels of service and training, and then supervising the case managers who would monitor care. Soon I found myself part of a management team. Because of my experience working within an HMO, and my interest in teaching, I began to conduct workshops in Massachusetts and elsewhere for Biodyne. I also became involved in marketing issues, relationships with client organizations, and increasingly with medical policymaking. Gradually it became clear to me that I had not taken a linear step, the next logical one on my career path, but had drastically changed my career. Although the changes had been incremental, both the setting and my role were different in almost every respect from life in a staff-model HMO.

The differences between a publicly held managed care company and a staff-model HMO are significant. To begin with, the staff-model HMO of the 70s and 80s was an insulated and rather protective setting in which the experiment with population-based care proceeded for the practitioner and midlevel manager relatively free from outside scrutiny. By contrast, my new role was interventionist, highly threatening to the professional community and extremely visible and public. Second, I had moved from a population base of 50,000 enrollees served by my health center to concerns about millions of insured lives. The scope became even broader as my role within my new company evolved.

A year after taking my new job, I was asked to extend my role and became a regional medical director. Two years after that, I was promoted to the corporate level. The company also changed. First it became public; then it began to grow and acquire subsidiaries; finally it was, itself, purchased by a pharmaceutical management company (Medco Containment Services), which was then purchased by Merck

Pharmaceuticals, only to be spun off later. My job expanded, and travel became part of my routine. For the second time in my career, the first in over 20 years, I found myself involved on the frontier. Each new day brought challenges to stretch beyond my experience, learn new aspects of the field, and keep up with my profession while learning a new one: the business of mental health care. I discovered the other side of my ambivalence about business and found myself working, for the first time in my career, outside a medical setting. After over 20 years of highly structured worklife, I had no schedule, no job description, no clear reporting lines, and no patients. What I found I did have, however, was a solid identity as a psychiatrist and as a physician and a strong commitment to making things work better. The timing was right, in that the company needed and valued what I had to offer. In 1994, having blurred the boundary between business and medicine, I found myself activating the third of the career choices I had faced as a young man, the legal profession, when I assumed responsibility for managing adverse incidents.

OBSERVATIONS

Managed care, at its most basic level, represents the introduction of an executive function into health care. The psychiatrist who works as a clinician within a managed system must learn to work collaboratively as part of a system, responsible to colleagues as well as to patients. The psychiatrist manager must also play a dual role: facing outward, as representative and interlocuter, part of the professional community yet seeking to transform it; facing inward, guiding policy so that it is compatible with core clinical values as well as core patient needs. The challenge is to maintain balance and a sense of perspective while in an environment dominated by pragmatism rather than ideology, an environment that is constantly in motion, constantly being transformed. The gyroscope, I am convinced, resides in the fundamentals of a good clinical education and a clear sense of professional identity built on work with patients.

Since I cannot present my own journey as a linear one, I expect further change as circumstances require or make possible. My path has not been a conventional one, and much of it has been fortuitous and unplanned. As I reflect on my current activities, however, they feel in harmony with my values, talents, and interests. Should they cease to be so, I know that I can make further change. The essence of career fulfillment, I believe, is to recognize the unique combination of self and environment which provides sustenance, but to understand that no choice is permanent and life is fundamentally about managing change. As I learned in the second grade, good management and sustenance go hand in hand.

REFERENCES AND RECOMMENDED READING

Bennett, M. J. (1988), The greening of the HMO: Implications for prepaid psychiatry. *Amer. J. Psychiat.*, 145:1544–1549.
Bennett, M. J. (1993), View from the bridge: Reflections of a recovering staff model HMO psychiatrist. *Psychiat. Quart.*, 64:45–75
Dostoevski, F. (1943), Notes from the underground. In: *A Treasury of Russian Literature*, ed. B. Guerney. New York: Vanguard Press, pp. 437–538.
Lazarus, A. (1994), Opportunities for psychiatrists in managed care organizations. *Hosp. Community Psychiat.*, 45:1206–1210.

❊ 6 ❊

Why Choose an Academic Career?

[ACADEMIA]

Michelle B. Riba

Dr. Riba is the Director of Resident and Fellow Education in the Department of Psychiatry at the University of Michigan Medical Center. Dr. Riba
has also been the Vice-Chair of the APA Scientific Program Committee since
1991. She serves on the executive councils of Association for Academic
Psychiatry and of the American Association of Directors of Psychiatric
Residency Training. She is coeditor of Volumes 11–16 of the *Review of
Psychiatry* and has written extensively on topics related to residency training, managed care, and medication backup. Dr. Riba received her B.A. in
chemistry from Queens College; M.S. in organic chemistry from St. John's
University; and her M.D. from the University of Connecticut, where she also
completed her residency training in psychiatry.

Looking back on where I came from and where I am now, I wish I
could tell you that the steps I took were all carefully planned and well
thought out, that from early on I had a dream of what I wanted to do
and the rest of my life consisted of fulfilling this dream. I always have
admired people who were focused and knew exactly what they
wanted to be or do from an early age. In stark contrast to what I
admire, the best way to summarize my professional life would be to
say that I have had a lot of experiences, that I have seized
opportunities when they were presented, and that I am now able to
draw on my past to help in the present work that I do as a clinical
academician. This is not what I would necessarily advocate for
everyone, but it is what happened to me.

BACKGROUND

Certain themes have held importance for me and shaped my outlook. Growing up in the 50s and 60s in New York City with a mother who had a high-level position in the Social Security Administration, I was acutely aware of the lack of good child-care opportunities for working women and of the stigma and social isolation that befell women who were trying to raise a family and have a career out of choice. My interest in child-care issues, both professional and personal, continues into the 1990s, for, although things have changed since my mother's days, unfortunately, they haven't changed all that much. Graduating from college in 1970, my friends had various aspirations: to become "pinned or laveliered" sometime in college; to get an Mrs. degree as well as a B.A. (it seemed, sometimes, that the former was more important than the latter); to become a teacher perhaps. In fact, probably bowing to peer pressure, I gave up an inclination to go to medical school and became a high school science teacher instead. Very few women were going to medical school in those days, and I took the path of least resistance. Being part of a peer group and acknowledging the importance of friendship were positive aspects of this developmental phase.

Teaching high school science was probably my most difficult job. Writing five new lesson plans daily; preparing laboratory experiments; working with children with different levels of interest, intelligence, and behavioral abilities; working with parents with varying needs and commitment to their children's education; grading students' work and giving timely evaluations and constructive feedback to students – all made teaching a big challenge. I remember those days and appreciate what it means to be a good teacher. One of my interests as a training director today stems from this early teaching experience: we must help our residents learn to teach, since both teaching medical students, other residents, patients, and families is a large part of what we do as psychiatrists, especially those of us in academics, and learning how to give timely evaluations and constructive criticism to our trainees are invaluable parts of the teaching and training process.

I met my future husband while in college (I guess I did succeed in obtaining an Mrs. as well as a B.A. after all!), and we moved to Philadelphia in 1973 for his residency. I became an environmental chemist for the Naval Facilities Engineering Command and also was named as Federal Women's Program Director. Part of the time I was training sewage treatment plant operators to monitor effluents for various pollutants, and the other part was spent helping to organize Upward Mobility and Affirmative Action Programs to help improve the career paths for civilian women in the Navy. This was quite a dual role! I continued to direct a Federal Women's Program for the Naval Underwater Systems Center in New London, Connecticut, when we moved there for my husband's fellowship. Not coincidentally, one of my first tasks at NUSC was to compile a handbook with all the local child-care opportunities that would be available for employees. This task clearly stemmed from my early view that the lack of excellent child care was a major deterrent to women's achieving their rightful places in the business world.

By now, my husband was in cardiology training at Yale. I was commuting an hour to New London, and I had a two-year-old daughter. I felt like a juggler who was trying to keep a lot of balls in the air and always worrying that one would fall. I tried working part-time for a while and thought that that was very difficult. I was always feeling that I should be at work—since I was missing meetings—or at home—because I was missing important events. At the same time, I was not getting paid in full, had fewer benefits, and wondered how in the world I could survive all this. When an interesting opportunity opened up closer to home, I took it. I was still an employee of the Navy, but the National Science Foundation sponsored me to work for a local organization, the Connecticut Conference of Municipalities, a lobbying organization for cities and towns. The goal of this demonstration project was to see if such placements could help put some of the expertise and know-how of federal employees into local situations. The project was called Technology Transfer. I learned about the workings of local and state politics, met key government officials, and discovered how to get a bill through the state legislature (or to stop one from being passed). I organized major state-wide conferences on various Technology Transfer topics and even edited a bulletin for government officials about ways to save money and use technology more productively.

I was 32 and had gone through several career changes and wondered if I really wanted to keep moving from one opportunity to another without a real plan. I decided to go back to school. I can still remember how difficult it was to study biochemistry and gross anatomy with a four-year-old daughter in tow. Even in 1981, very few of my medical school classmates were married or had children.

Although I wanted more children, I knew I couldn't manage adding to our family while in medical school. Even though we were able to afford in-house child care, it was still emotionally difficult for me to be away from home so much. So it wasn't until I was a fourth-year psychiatry resident that our second daughter was born, 12 years younger than her sister. This was not exactly ideal spacing by most standards!

THE ROAD TO ACADEMICS

During residency training, I was fortunate to be mentored for a future career in academics. The training director at the University of Connecticut at the time, Allan Tasman, encouraged, advocated and supported various roles for me. One was as chair of the resident group in our department. The other was as a representative to the APA Committee of Residents and Fellows (CORF). It was through the link with the CORF that I began to meet residents from throughout the country. We worked on many projects that I think benefited other trainees and strengthened their role in the APA. One of the duties of the CORF was to edit the APA *Psychiatric Resident Newsletter* (PRN), which I did with another CORF member, Douglas Ziedonis, since I had had experience doing something similar in my previous career at the Connecticut Conference of Municipalities. This was another example of relying on my past to help in a present position. The CORF was a formative experience in my development and strengthens my conviction today of the important role that the APA plays in nurturing leadership in residents. Friends from those early days include Patricia Isbell, Tana Grady, and Doug Ziedonis, all of whom today are in academic departments of psychiatry. I raise friendship as an issue because the importance of this bonding and having a strong peer group is often understated in discussions of career development. Just as my college peer group had been so strong, so too was my new group of psychiatrist friends.

As time for graduation from the residency approached, a unique opportunity occurred at our training program. The University of Connecticut Psychiatry Residency Program was merging with the program at the Institute of Living. Dr. Tasman asked me to stay on as associate training director and Assistant Clinical Professor to help with this merger. Clinically, I started off working on the adult inpatient psychiatry unit of the John Dempsey Hospital and after one year moved to doing consultation-liaison psychiatry at the Hospital. The merger, including the strategies and process for change, offered some unique opportunities to write and speak at national meetings. Learning how to combine administrative and clinical tasks with the more academic duties of publishing and lecturing is an important survival skill in an academic career. Juggling all this became complex, especially as my children were growing up and family and personal demands (like taking care of myself, spending time with my spouse, keeping my house sort of semi-clean) march on.

Other professional opportunities that were very nurturing included joining the Association for Academic Psychiatry (AAP), which fostered important opportunities to be mentored by Carolyn Robinowitz, and Ellen Leibenluft. I now edit the Bulletin of the AAP – a job that seems natural following the other newsletters I've edited over the years. Mentors and friends who have played important roles in helping me stay on track with balancing my professional and personal goals include Leah Dickstein, Carol Nadelson, and John Oldham.

Clearly, having had mentors was important in my development. Additionally, having had prior experiences in such organizations as the Navy, as a teacher, and the like, also gave me the confidence to take on new roles as a resident and then as an academician.

My husband took a new position in Michigan, and our family moved again in 1993. I joined the faculty at the University of Michigan and am currently Assistant Clinical Professor and Director of the Psychiatry Residency and Fellow Program. Clinically, I am a consultation-liaison psychiatrist. I continue to be active in the APA and organizations such as the Association for Academic Psychiatry and the American Association of Directors of Psychiatric Residency Training. I have learned that belonging to national professional organizations really helps in the transition from one academic center to another. It takes a period of time to become known in a new academic institution. It is comforting, therefore, that no matter where one moves, the national professional organizations afford an opportunity for stability of friendships and fellowship.

ACADEMIC PSYCHIATRY

Here at the University of Michigan, residents, fellows, and even faculty members wonder if academic psychiatry will survive. That's a big question. Following from that, trainees, including medical students and residents, want to know if going into academic psychiatry is still a viable career path.

The fate of academic psychiatry departments is linked to the successful survival of academic medical centers (AMCs) (Riba and Carli, in press). Although there are 126 American medical schools, only about 61 university-owned teaching hospitals exist, and fewer than half of these are research intensive. This number keeps changing as teaching hospitals are being sold and bought by large conglomerates, with the character, style, and direction often shifting from an "academic" focus to a more entrepreneurial and business style. It is important to note that much of the medical student and resident education in psychiatry in this country occurs in nonuniversity-centered public and private hospitals.

One of the biggest challenges facing AMCs is that they now must compete in the marketplace while still adhering to their distinguishing feature—balancing the tripartite mission of education, research, and delivery of clinical services. Each of these missions is in the throes of enormous change and is often at odds with changes in the others. The fate of departments of psychiatry rests with the ability of AMCs to cohere and synthesize these various missions and market-driven tensions.

Central to the problem is that teaching and doing research cost money and time. As we try to move from medical education programs whose clinical experiences were based on inpatient units (where the patients used to be) to outpatient centers (where the patients are now), voids are left on the inpatient side that must be filled by faculty. More faculty resources now have to go into providing direct patient care.

This takes time away from traditional academic work—teaching and doing research. Faculty meetings in departments of psychiatry today sound more like business briefings: What new managed care contract did we lose or get? If we won the contract, now what—who is going to provide the service?

Faculty members in many AMCs must now generate upward of 80% of their salary either through clinical revenue or research funding. Research dollars are more difficult to obtain. In 1975, 40% of new investigator-initiated applications to NIH were funded. In 1990, that number dropped to 14.2% (Cadman, 1994). Resubmitted grant applications had a success rate of 70% in 1975, but only 35% in 1990 (Cadman, 1994). It is estimated that an investigator must submit six grant applications to get one funded and that obtaining stable funding from NIH requires writing a grant application every eight months (Cadman, 1994). As clinical loads build up, as research dollars grow scarce, as doom and gloom reports hover over AMCs, academicians begin to wonder what the attraction to an academic career is.

The problem is particularly difficult for the group of junior psychiatrists who are under the gun of the "tenure clock." They usually have five to seven years to secure a research path, establish external funding, and publish anywhere from 20 to 30 peer-reviewed papers. Although many universities have clinical/teaching tracks as well as the traditional tenure/research ones, promotion committees often operate under rules and values that have not fully acclimated to the clinical and fiscal urgencies of managed care issues. As the AMC comes to value and need the services of clinically able academic psychiatrists, it seems imperative to strengthen the position of such faculty in the department. As I prepare my own documentation for promotion this year, nowhere on the application form does the promotion committee ask how many patients I take care of or the quality of my clinical practice. There are, however, a lot of spaces for information about papers written, grants obtained, and programs and projects developed. And, at our university, those on the clinician/teacher track are not eligible for tenure. The good news, however, is that clinicians are often paid on a higher salary schedule than are those on the academic/tenure tracks. I predict that, in the future, the role of the clinican/teacher academic psychiatrist will become increasingly important in the survival of AMCs and departments of psychiatry. Whether clinician/teachers at most academic institutions will be granted academic parity (tenure) is questionable.

One of the darker clouds hovering over us has to do with the viability of psychiatry as a field. Health care delivery is changing and increasingly includes intermediary companies and businesses that manage care for a profit. Managed care emphasizes cost and efficiency, sometimes at the expense of quality of care (Tischler, 1990; Gabbard, 1992) and intrudes on the doctor–patient relationship (Sabin, 1991). Although these issues affect all medical disciplines, they hit particularly hard on psychiatry, which so values this relationship. All this comes at a time when there is an increased emphasis on primary care in medical school education. Recruitment of senior medical students into primary care disciplines is growing, especially as job opportunities seem to be predominantly in these areas, with fewer in subspecialties such as psychiatry.

Another critical factor to contend with is that funding sources for psychiatry residency positions are also changing. Historically, postgraduate medical education had been subsidized through a variety of mechanisms involving cost distributions between public and private health insurance plans that financed the care of covered patients (Tasman, 1993). The pattern of such reimbursement has changed in the last decade (Relman, 1984; Schwartz, Newhouse, and Williams, 1985), most residency programs are no longer able to cover completely direct and indirect costs of resident stipends through these reimbursement mechanisms.

Many psychiatric educators are noting that the future of psychiatry is indeed uncertain given the changes in health care delivery combined with the shifting values and premiums being placed on primary care. Some, like Gabbard (1992), note that the transition from residency to practice is a "nightmare" because of the lack of education and training in managed care principles being given to residents. Sabin (1993) comments that residents are not being adequately prepared for postresidency practice because academic psychiatrists have "moral myopia" regarding managed care principles. Many of the faculty who are teaching residents were not themselves trained in those principles and so need to be educated how best to survive within the framework of managed care. They seem ill equipped to act as role models, supervisors, and teachers of medical students and residents. In our own training program, we often find residents explaining to their teachers and supervisors such issues as how to arrange for different levels of care, insurance, and managed care rules governing treatment options; which forms to fill out for which type of health care policy; and so on. The issue of the viability of academic psychiatry is part of the larger question of the viability of psychiatry as a field.

Although psychiatry has not been declared a primary-care specialty, psychiatrists of the future may increasingly be asked to watch over their patients' nonpsychiatric medical illnesses. More training programs are being developed between psychiatry and primary care in which psychiatrists work directly with physicians and patients in the outpatient primary-care settings.

Another view is that psychopharmacology will be a principal task of the psychiatrist. As other professions provide a bigger chunk of the psychotherapy needs of patients, psychiatrists may find themselves increasingly in the role of providing medication coverage or backup to their nonphysician colleagues (Hansen-Grant and Riba, 1995). Residency training programs are modifying curricula and clinical experiences to reflect these changing roles in the hope of keeping their residents employable and optimally trained upon graduation. Other ways that programs are changing include shifting residents' experiences from inpatient to outpatient clinical sites, electives or rotations to health maintenance organizations, education about managed care principles and the business side of medical practice, and teaching residents about outcomes research data and how to interpret such information.

CONCLUSION

Transitions and changes in psychiatry are affecting multiple levels of academia—medical students' and residents' training and perceptions about psychiatry; recruitment into our field; clinical workloads on faculty; success of academic careers as measured by research, teaching, and clinical productivity; and patient flow into AMCs as affected by marketplace forces. With tripartite missions in a department (clinical, research, and education) and multiple players (trainees, clinical faculty, researchers, and educators), it is no wonder that there is a domino effect: a shift or change in one area leads to similar or worse problems down the line.

I think the future for academic psychiatry continues to be bright. There will always be a need for psychiatric and neuroscience research. Obviously, the biggest questions concern who will pay for this, how competitive obtaining funds will be, and how many clinical and teaching hours researchers will have to provide within a given department of psychiatry. The future of clinical academic psychiatry is also very bright. As health care reform moves AMCs more into center stage in the marketplace, the value and importance of clinical psychiatrists who can also teach and do some clinical research will continue to be realized. I am optimistic when residents ask if there is value in planning for a career in academic psychiatry.

What is critical to the future of academic psychiatry relates to how we ready ourselves for present and future changes, how we continue to be flexible in a chaotic marketplace, and, finally, how we determine that medical students' and residents' training needs aren't shortchanged as faculty are asked to take on larger clinical and teaching loads.

On the basis of my own experiences, I appreciate and encourage residents who have had other careers before coming to medicine, who have other interests and responsibilities and would like armchair advice in figuring how to juggle it all, and who enjoy new opportunities in their own career development and enhancement. I hope that I have learned from my mentors how to be a role model and mentor for junior members of our profession. Being a residency training director affords me a perfect opportunity to use my experiences and love of teaching, clinical care, and mentorship in a setting of academic psychiatry. I continue to juggle the various dimensions of my life. I'm more relaxed now when the balls fall, and I have a bit less anticipatory anxiety worrying about the juggling act not working. Still, a career in clinical academic psychiatry offers a unique and positive opportunity for those interested in teaching, research, and clinical care while also raising a family.

REFERENCES

Cadman, E. D. (1994), The academic physician-investigator: A crisis not to be ignored. *Ann. Int. Med.*, 120:401–410.

Gabbard, G. (1992), The big chill: The transition from residency to managed care nightmare. *Acad. Psychiat.*, 16:119–126.

Hansen-Grant, S. & Riba, M. (1995), Contact between psychotherapists and psychiatric residents who provide medication backup. *Psychiat. Serv.*, 46:774–777.

Relman, A. S. (1984), Who will pay for medical education in our teaching hospitals? *Science*, 226:20–23.

Riba, M. & Carli, T. (in press), Will academic psychiatry survive managed care? In: *Controversies in Managed Mental Health Care*, ed. A. Lazarus. Washington, DC: American Psychiatric Press.

Sabin, J. E. (1991), The therapeutic alliance in managed care mental health practice. *J. of Psychother. Prac. and Res.*, 1:29–36.

Schwartz, W. B., Newhouse, J. P., & Williams, A. P. (1985), Is the teaching hospital an endangered species? *New Eng. J. Med.*, 313:157–162.

Tasman, A. & Riba, M. (1993), Strategic issues for the successful merger of residency training programs. *Hosp. Commun. Psychiat.*, 44:981–985.

Tischler, G. L. (1990), Utilization management and the quality of care. *Hosp. Commun. Psychiat.*, 41:1099–1102.

⚜ 7 ⚜

The Inveterate NIMH Career Researcher: The Opportunities and Perils of Clinical Research in the Intramural Program

[RESEARCH]

Robert M. Post

Dr. Post is Chief of the Biological Psychiatry Branch, National Institute of Mental Health in Bethesda, Maryland. He is widely known for his research in mood disorders and has devoted his career to the study of behavioral and biochemical alterations during ill and well states of patients. Dr. Post's seminal research on the kindling phenomenon helped revolutionize research in and treatment approaches to bipolar disorder. A prolific author and lecturer, Dr. Post has published nearly 600 articles and book chapters. Dr. Post is the associate editor of *Psychiatry Research* and serves on the editorial boards of numerous scientific journals. He is the recipient of the Selo Award for Reasearch in Affective Illness from NARSAD, the Gerald L. Klerman Lifetime Research Award for his research in manic-depressive illness from the National Depressive Manic-Depressive Association, and the Nathaniel William Winkelman Award from the Belmont Center for Comprehensive Treatment in Philadelphia, Pennsylvania.

PRE-NIMH

I arrived at my current position as Chief of the Biological Psychiatry Branch of the National Institute of Mental Health through a somewhat improbable and circuitous route. I grew up in New Haven, Connecticut, with the only real academic goal of leaving my hometown and not going to school at Yale University. However, my general practitioner, who was also a "townie," persuaded me to apply to Yale on the grounds that home life would not interfere with academic life, and, upon early admission, I was persuaded that filling out a lot of other complicated application forms was not a worthwhile endeavor.

So, I became a "townie" and took up studies in psychology at Yale (1960–1964) with the idea I had adopted in high school that a career as a physician was a not unworthy goal. Psychology and the brain sciences appeared to be one of the most vast and wide open frontiers in medicine; they combined the chance to help individuals as a physician with unique opportunities for new discoveries. It seemed that people knew the basics of how the heart and kidneys worked, but virtually nothing about the neurobiology of the brain. Certainly, almost anyone with some degree of curiosity could make a worthwhile contribution in this area.

Thus motivated and excited by an early talk on the wild nature of brain activity during REM sleep by Robert Galambos, and on the fundamentals of learning, memory, and behavior by critical method-ologist Fred Sheffield, I completed an undergraduate honors thesis on the role of empathy and projection as a function of self-esteem. I asked best friends to rate themselves and the other on a Q-sort for their self and ideal. Self-esteem was measured by how close to one's ideal self one was on a "self Q-sort," and empathy was a measure of how close one could estimate one's best friend's self-rated Q-sort. Clinical research seemed like an interesting endeavor.

I attended medical school at the University of Pennsylvania School of Medicine (1964–1968), where my physiology professor Jerry Smith made me write a paper on a most ludicrous-sounding topic at the time—the role of the limbic system in appetite and other appetitive functions. This was obviously a silly proposition on the face of it, since this part of the brain was certainly a long way from the stomach, and it was quite clear that the hypothalamus was the major player in the control of these appetitive drive states, in any event. Thus, armed with an appropriate combination of ignorance and ridicule, I was set onto a topic that I have never quite abandoned in my adult research career at the NIMH—that is, the role of limbic and higher cortical brain systems in the regulation of emotion in normal and pathological mood states.

In medical school I was totally amazed that you could actually see such things as an amoeba through a microscope, but I had much less success in organic chemistry in identifying an unknown chemical that was supposedly present in an otherwise clear, watery fluid. I learned every muscle and bone in the body but called an obvious pair of ovaries in a cadaver seminal vesicles on our final exam in anatomy – I knew that this was obviously wrong, but somehow I could not quite make the transition from the male cadaver I had dissected (which clearly had nothing like these ovaries in it) to what might be a female, and so seminal vesicles seemed as good a choice as any.

Despite these minor blind spots regarding the differences between men and women, Richard Harner welcomed me into his neurology-neuropsychology lab as a fledgling medical student. By these and a series of other encouragements and opportunities, Penn turned any number of us on as not only clinicians but academic physicians. My roommate was Stan Prusiner, before he was displaced by my wife, Susan. Prusiner went on to elucidate the role of prions in neurodegenerative and infectious disease processes. Until just a year or two ago, many in the scientific community ridiculed him for the outrageous proposition that something smaller than a virus could be the cause of their illness; they knew it had to be a slow virus, even though none was found.

Off to Albert Einstein School of Medicine in the Bronx (1968–1969) because of its unique neurology-medicine-pediatrics intern rotation, which seemed to be the most appropriate preparation for a career in psychiatry. A dizzying year of introduction to psychopathology at Massachusetts General (1969–1970) was cut short of a full residency because of an offer from Biff Bunney to go to the NIMH two years early because a slot had suddenly become vacant and the offer was definite at that time and uncertain for the future at the completion of my residency. After a minor glitch following the statement from the FBI that I was not a suitable enough American to join the Public Health Service (perhaps because I had joined in the March on Washington or some other criminal activity of which I am not aware to this date) and the intervention of my brother-in-law and the American Civil Liberties Union, I arrived in the hallowed halls of the Intramural Program of the NIMH for an intended two-year clinical fellowship in the PHS (1970–1972). I was most pleased to have my

Service obligations fulfilled thusly so that I would not have to partake in the Vietnam experience. While I always knew I wanted to go into academic medicine, this would likely have been in a university setting if it were not for the PHS opportunity for further research training in the context of a military exemption. (One wonders how much the absence of this type of motivating factor, following the termination of mandatory draft requirements, has played a role in the diminishing number of applicants to the Intramural Program.)

NIMH (1970–1995)

Clinical Associateship

Upon my arrival at the NIMH, Biff Bunney, Fred Goodwin, and Dennis Murphy met with me and, to my horror, asked me what I wanted to study. I replied I had no idea. When pressed, I still could not conjure up anything but said I'd be willing to help out in any ongoing work. Fred, Biff, and Dennis then drew straws to decide who was going to get stuck with this obvious loser. Fred drew me, and he and Biff suggested that I study whether cocaine had antidepressant effects in order to "test" the catecholamine hypothesis of depression that Bunney, Schildkraut, Davis, and others had recently posited as a counter to the European and Prange-ian serotonin permissive hypothesis of depression. Again, I was faced with what appeared to be a patently silly idea, but, not having any other option in mind (especially since I did not yet know exactly where levodopa and tyrosine hydroxylase fit into the catecholaminergic biosynthetic pathway), I reluctantly said O.K. I comforted myself with the thought that, even if I did not make a convincing statement regarding the catecholamine hypothesis, the research offered the opportunity to administer a drug to depressed patients that was a euphoriant and mood elevator in normals, and see if they would feel better.

I was struck with the findings that most depressed patients did not have pure euphoric responses to cocaine, and, in fact, the majority had some type of dysphoric activation. Moreover, all attempts to try to "capture" positive acute clinical responses, in those few individuals who showed them, for long-term clinical benefit were unsuccessful with the use of repeated intravenous, oral, and subcutaneous administration. In fact, some patients appeared to deteriorate rather than improve following initial positive responses.

These early clinical observations then opened up a series of themes for me as a first-year clinical associate, and I have been studying them further and revisiting them periodically over the past 25 years of my NIMH career:

1) Acute response to a given manipulation in normals does not necessarily occur in a similar fashion in depressed patients (a theme revisited with the observations of the antidepressant effects of sleep deprivation in depressed patients but not normal volunteers).

2) Even positive acute manipulations in patients are not easily converted to long-term clinical antidepressant efficacy (a theme repeatedly visited with sleep deprivation, amphetamine infusions, levodopa infusions, 5-HTP, threo-dops, and, more recently, thyrotropin-releasing hormone [TRH] administration).

3) Acute effects of a drug may be very different from those following long-term administration, either to the benefit or to the detriment of the intended effect. (a) The chronic effects of cocaine became more interesting than the acute effects and led to the exploration of the themes of behavioral sensitization and reverse tolerance as opposed to tolerance as the "only" motive adaptation to long-term psychotropic drug treatment. (b) Not only did cocaine induce progressive increases in hyperactivity, stereotypy, hyperthermia, and catatonia following repetition of the same dose administered to a variety of experimental animals, but, remarkably, some animals began to develop seizures with a dose of cocaine that was subconvulsant.

Thus, a venture into the early preclinical literature on chronic cocaine administration opened entirely new vistas of mechanisms underlying increased pathological, behavioral, and physiological responsivity with repeated stimulation or drug administration. I became aware of Graham Goddard's paper in 1969 on the development of amygdala-kindled seizures upon repeated stimulation of the amygdala as part of an experiment he intended to do on learning and memory. Despite his best efforts, Goddard could not avoid many of the animals' developing seizures in response to a previously subconvulsant stimulation current, and his wise thesis advisor, Lashley, told him to abandon his initial thesis objective and study the pathophysiological mechanisms involved in this much more interesting phenomenon of kindling.

(c) The parallelism between cocaine-kindled seizures and amygdala-kindled seizures induced electrically in the Goddard-Racine-Wada paradigmatic mode appeared all too appealing and obvious to me, and I now reluctantly accept responsibility for contaminating the pure concept of kindling achieved electrically by the Canadians with that induced by pharmacological probes, such as cocaine, lidocaine, and procaine. Adding even more to my permanent placement in academic purgatory was the notion, so elegantly pioneered by Bob Adamec and Everett Ellinwood, that this type of kindling-like progression of symptomatology could be relevant to the unfolding of pathological behavior in a variety of neuropsychiatric syndromes.

4) Chronic effects of drugs are pertinent to the time-course of therapeutic actions of the psychotropic agents, and the longitudinal approach to illness development may reveal many different types of physiological secrets beyond the acute hypotheses of episode dysfunction underlying the classical catecholamine hypothesis. For example, most antidepressants require two to three weeks to exert their maximal therapeutic effects (although onset is often within the first week).

5) Intermittency and chronicity can produce relatively opposite effects on biochemistry and behavior. One of the more important determinants of whether end-points sensitize versus tolerate is the pattern of exposure. This principle appears to be the key driving force underlying both sensitization and kindling because of their intermittency and may, as well, be fundamental to the distinction between long-term potentiation (LTP) and long-term depression (LTD). Most recently, Susan Weiss and I have used LTD-like parameters in order to block the development of kindling and reverse it once it has become fully manifest in a phenomenon we now call "quenching." Thus, key elements of kindling versus quenching are the frequency, duration, and pattern of stimulation, including intermittency.

6) It's hard to ignore the "dreaded" limbic system that Jerry Smith so sagaciously ordered onto my pallet. It turned out that the local anesthetic components of cocaine were highly limbic-selective. Data were highly suggestive, based on electrophysiological measures in the literature, but had not been definitively proven. Given the newly available deoxyglucose technique pioneered by Sokoloff, Kennedy,

and their colleagues, we examined the effects of lidocaine-kindled seizures in rodents with them and confirmed that they selectively activated the limbic system. Terence A. Ketter and his colleagues (1993) then went on to confirm this limbic selectivity with low doses of procaine in man.

7) The limbic theme also directly propelled us to a new therapeutic modality: we explored the anticonvulsant carbamazepine for its effects in primary affective disorders. We chose to examine carbamazepine because of its relative limbic selectivity. Not only did it inhibit amygdala-kindled seizures compared with cortical-kindled seizures better than any of the existing anticonvulsants, but its use in the epilepsies was often associated with reports of positive effects on mood and affect in those patients with secondary affective disorders. After we had initiated our search for such a limbic preferential probe, we became aware of Okuma, Kishimoto, and Inoue's (1975) studies in Japan reporting positive effects of carbamazepine in primary affective illness in open clinical trials in the early 1970s.

Third-year Fellowship and Beyond

At the end of the two-year fellowship it was obvious that a third year would be very helpful to finish up clinical research on basic projects that had been initiated in the first two years. A third year was highly productive under the continued tutelage of Fred Goodwin and additional oversight by Biff Bunney and Irv Kopin. I could even pursue a project in neurosurgery, following up on my work with Richard Harner in neurology at the University of Pennsylvania School of Medicine. There I had learned to perform the isolated forebrain preparations of Villablanca in the cat and found that the disconnected forebrain would go into REM sleep at different times from the rest of the brain. At the NIMH I also escaped from the complexities and stresses of the clinical research unit to the animal neurosurgical suite. I did laminectomies on monkeys in order to gain access to the cerebroventricular system. I also performed studies of CSF dynamics with injection of radio-labeled isotopes into primates by shaking them upside down in order to examine the effects of activity and position on CSF flow after wheedling my way with an anesthetized primate into the human neuroradiology suite. The primates were well bundled during the transport from Building 9 to Building 10, to protect them not only from the cold, but also from visual inspection by curious patients and staff members.

I studied catecholamine metabolites in CSF of patients with affective illness and found them low in the 1970s, when patients were more classically depressed and it was fashionable to observe such findings in depressed patients compared with either manics or normal volunteer controls. (Later, patients presenting with more anxious depression tended to show higher levels of CSF norepinephrine and its metabolite MHPG.)

A series of lessons in not following conventional wisdom continued to intrude. As I was attempting to understand the origin of the CSF amine metabolites that we were studying in affectively ill patients, I decided to use the flexibility of the Intramural Research Program and travel to the VA system to study patients with spinal cord transections in order to assess the contribution of the spinal cord versus that of high areas of brain in such CSF studies. I was informed by several neurological colleagues that such a study would be both undoable and ill fated. Since such advice was not followed by a line of reasoning that I could understand, I persisted in these studies and made the transition from an undoable and uninterpretable study to one that could be published in *Science*.

The Intramural Program supported such flexibility and opportunism as well as providing positive mentorship and support without my having to prove the legitimacy of a good idea to disbelieving and constitutionally conservative reviewers, particularly in the absence of preliminary data to support such a "grantlike" proposal. This revelation was to be encountered repeatedly and reexperienced throughout my 25 years at the NIMH, not only as a clinical fellow, research fellow, Unit Chief, Section Chief, and Laboratory Chief, but even (heaven forbid!) as a reviewer myself. I remember thinking that the idea that Carleton Gajdusek was looking for an infectious agent to explain kuru was silly. He won the Nobel Prize for this work, even though my college roommate, Stan Prusiner, found out it was really prions. I also remember thinking how foolish it was for Phil Gold to make a career change to study corticotropin-releasing factor (CRH) when this appeared to be somehow not quite as relevant as it now is in the pathophysiology of affective disorders.

A wonderful asset of the Intramural Program is that it allows one to choose among many options after two or three years' fellowship. At the end of my third-year fellowship, I was offered outstanding opportunities at Yale and the University of Pittsburgh. Locked in an obsessional crisis of the worst kind of approach–approach conflict, I opted to stay put in an environment that had been most reinforcing, with which I had some familiarity, and where I knew that I could at least navigate around its major obstacles. Biff Bunney and Bob Cohen, then Clinical Director of NIMH, helped put together a clinical research position, developing an Affective Disorders Unit on 3-West, which had formerly been involved only in psychosocial studies of adolescents. My first two Clinical Associates, Fred Stoddard and John Carman, taught me much about initiating a patient and staff community into the clinical research adventure after the model of Fred Goodwin, Dennis Murphy, and Biff Bunney. Fred cultivated excellence and taught me the lesson that no amount of time was too much to spend on helping to make a manuscript or illustration as readable and near perfect as possible (my apologies to the readers of this one, however). Biff taught me the fortitude to pursue novel ideas, and about loyalty to colleagues and supervisees.

The primary rule of NIMH was to invite highly motivated clinical fellows into the program and let them pursue their ideas even when they seemed foolhardy. Thus, when I got to be a Unit Chief and attempted to mentor and be mentored by John Carman, I somewhat reluctantly allowed him to pursue his then bizarre-sounding themes of the role of calcium in the affective disorders and, even more astonishingly and incongruous appearing at the time, the role of dopamine agonists in depression. (Everyone knew that the catecholamine, norepinephrine, and perhaps the indoleamine serotonin were the only really important candidates to pursue.) Rocky Gerner soon followed with even more preposterous ideas about the role of GABA in depression, a theme he pursued after leaving NIMH, and he was the first to report, along with another clinical fellow David Rubinow, low somatostatin in the CSF of depressed patients. This finding of low CSF somatostatin in depression, along with hypercortisolism, appears to be one of the most highly replicated findings in the neurobiology of the affective disorders.

John Carman's ideas of more than 20 years ago have never left the thematic exploration of our laboratory, and we have now circled back to explore not only the role of traditional psychotropic medications and the anticonvulsants on calcium metabolism, but also the calcium channel blockers themselves, such as nimodipine and isradipine. The dihydropyridine L-type calcium channel blockers nimodipine and isradipine appear to be highly effective in a subgroup of patients with refractory affective illness (even those who do not respond to the more traditional L-type calcium channel blocker verapamil). Carman's exploration of the dopamine agonist ET-495 (piribedil) presaged the work with bromocriptine and other dopamine agonists, including recent work with the reuptake blockers nomifensine and amineptine (approved in France) as well as the atypical antidepressant bupropion, with its interesting ability to increase dopamine in the nucleus accumbens and striatum. Surprisingly, all the classical antidepressants also appear to increase mesolimbic dopamine responsivity, as does ECT.

Carman's legacy in helping to propel two ridiculous ideas into the mainstream of the clinical therapeutics of the affective disorders—focusing on calcium and dopamine—stand as a wonderful marker of the opportunities of novel clinical research ideas within the Intramural Program. (Sadly, under the increased federal budget shortfall and attendant increased scrutiny by an ever-growing list of review panels from within and without, many such novel ideas are being squelched in the rigidification and multiplication of the review process.) More and more, intramural investigators, like their overburdened extramural colleagues, are being told to present simple and thematically continuous ideas for review and save "the good stuff" for surreptitious conduct on the side. We can only hope that, as the catecholamine and indoleamine hypotheses of the affective disorders cycle in and out of prominence, modern-day political peculiarities in the review process will eventually be ameliorated.

The success of the Intramural Program is attested to not only by some of us who have remained, but by the ascendency and productivity of those who have left. The major professorial chairs and chairmanships of many of the departments of psychiatry throughout the country are populated by former clinical associates of the Intramural Program. Virtually any clinical associate can merit a first-rate academic job, and the best among them can easily move to tenured professorships or departmental chairs. A modern-day Jim Ballenger,

Russ Joffe, Ned Kalin, and Tom Uhde match up with a Jan Fawcett, Biff Bunney, Dave Janowsky, and John Davis. Those such as a Mark George, Terence Ketter, Peter Roy-Byrne, Tom Insel, Barbara Parry, Husseini Manji, and Lori Altshuler match the "older" generation of David Jimerson, Robert Gerner, Victor Reus, Gabriella Carlson, Craig Risch, Chris Gillin, and the like.

Outsiders occasionally comment on the competitiveness of the Intramural Program, but this should not be mistaken for a lack of collegiality. Compared with some of the stories I have heard in some academic departments around the country, the Intramural Program appears to be relatively well off in this regard. In fact, the potential for interesting and productive collaborative relationships both within the NIMH and even across institutes is one of the most exciting aspects of the Intramural Program. Perhaps toleration of novel and weird ideas breeds a certain amount of tolerance for those of us who share these same liabilities as personality traits.

Laboratory Chief at NIMH

When I became Section Chief, many of my Lab Chief colleagues told me that I would never have it as good again. Perhaps they were right. Freedom to pursue one's ideas in both the clinical and the preclinical laboratories were unparalleled and almost completely unfettered by the now-increasing administrative and political preoccupations of a Lab Chief. As a Unit and Section Chief working with a series of wonderful Clinical Associate colleagues, I helped introduce carbamazepine into general clinical practice as an alternative to lithium for refractory bipolar patients and performed more than 150 studies on its clinical and preclinical mechanisms of action and laboratory effects and side effects.

We were soon faced, however, with the distressing reality that, increasingly, patients were presenting to our clinical research unit already prescreened for lithium and carbamazepine refractoriness. We began to pursue some of the alternatives with thyroid augmentation strategies, valproate, and a variety of combination strategies that were highly effective in allowing us to discharge some three-quarters of patients either completely well or moderately to markedly improved (as rated on the clinical global impression [CGI] scale). We began to assess the efficacy of the L-type calcium channel blocker nimodipine and also found it important to some of the therapeutic successes as we have attempted to match clinical research with therapeutics. In some instances we found that the combination of two and three mood stabilizers with an antidepressant or thyroid augmentation were necessary for getting patients well.

If one stays at the NIMH long enough and is persistent and stubborn enough, all sorts of clinical research obstacles can be overcome. Intravenous procaine studies in humans started by Frank Putnam and Charlie Kellner more than 10 years ago were taken up by Mitch Kling and, most recently, Terry Ketter. Dr. Ketter verified procaine as a limbic-selective probe, imaged the brains of 32 normal volunteers with O^{15} PET, and documented that procaine activated the amygdala and its outflow pathways into the insula, orbital frontal cortex, and anterior cingulate gyrus. This was associated with a variety of psychosensory alterations and either profound euphoria or dysphoria. This gives a remarkable hint into a possible neural substrate of affective dysregulation in bipolar illness as limbic-selective activation, even in normal volunteers, can produce relatively opposite effects on mood. Ketter also showed that those with visual hallucinations had increased blood flow in the visual (occipital) cortex, presenting one of the first brain imaging road maps of pathways activated during a visual hallucination. With other PET studies he also found evidence of both frontal cortical and limbic alterations in patients with the affective disorders. Consistent with the data from a large number of other studies in primary and secondary depression, Ketter and his colleagues found that the degree of decrement in left frontal lobe metabolism correlated with the severity of depression measured on Hamilton Ratings.

Partially on the basis of these observations, another Clinical Associate, Mark George, began attempts to modify directly the metabolism of this area of the brain using repeated transcranial magnetic stimulation (rTMS). As a Clinical Associate, I had conducted a series of studies on the simulation of motor activity of mania as a partial control for assessing whether such activity could drive up CSF amine metabolites independent of mood disorder. As a senior investigator I suggested that Mark George pursue another simulation, that of sadness induction, in order to assess the potential areas of brain normally involved in the modulation of affect as a partial control for some of the confounds that might be involved in imaging pathological mood states such as depression. The normal volunteers in the sadness induction (remembering a past sad event, getting into that mood, and viewing an affect-appropriate face) activated paralimbic and, particularly, left frontal cortical areas compared with a neutral condition or a happiness induction. Remarkably, women activated seven times more brain substance in their sadness compared with their happiness induction or compared with men in either induction. While much work remains to elucidate the reasons for this differential activation of brain in women, these preliminary data are suggestive of interesting gender differences in the cerebral correlates of (sad/happiness) mood induction, which were rated as equally profound subjectively by the men and the women. Depressed patients appeared to have more difficulty accessing these differential mood states and, again, showed relative hyporesponsivity in many areas compared with controls. In addition to completing the study conceived several years ago, Mark George was able to carry out a much more remarkable feat in applying an entirely new technology (rTMS) to attempt to open new fields of therapeutics in the neuropsychiatric illnesses.

More than 20 years ago, after watching one of the first U.S. space walks, I remarked on the incredible rapidity with which the science fiction of my youth—Buck Rogers taking a space walk—was transformed into scientific reality. I wondered what might be in store for us in this regard in the neurosciences and wrote a short and appropriately preposterous paper predicting the advances that could be in the offing in the future. The paper was preliminarily entitled "The Future of the Brain and Its Prospects in the Next Century" (with the full intent to retitle it in a more presentable, less pretentious fashion). I never could think up a good title for the paper, so it was never submitted for publication. I was remarkably chagrined, however, to find out that predictions that had been projected for decades in the future were already coming true while the ink was still drying. These included neuronal implants for Parkinson's Disease and gene therapy for a variety of medical illnesses, as well as the ability to influence, in an up- or down-regulating fashion, electrical activity in discrete areas of brain by focal electromagnetic stimulation. Little did I know that Mark George in my laboratory would actually bring this 21st-century dream into reality in 1994–1995.

Dr. George, in collaboration with colleagues in the Neurology Institute, has pioneered the use of rTMS for the treatment of mood disorders. When a magnetic coil is placed over the motor cortex, motor potentials and motor jerking movements of the hand can be repetitively produced. Depending on the intensity of stimulation, this can be made to occur below motor thresholds. Based on the finding of left frontal lobe hypometabolism in depressed patients and the finding that rTMS differentially affected mood in normal volunteers with left and right prefrontal cortical stimulation, Dr. George used rTMS over the left prefrontal cortex of our depressed patients. In two of the first six, he found remarkable degrees of antidepressant response, including the induction of a complete remission in one patient who had not been well for three years and had failed more than 10 different psychopharmacological antidepressant regimens. Two and a half months after her discharge from the NIMH this patient experienced a depressive recurrence and was again treated with rTMS with success and the achievement of another period of remission. Double-blind, randomized, controlled studies are now ongoing with this noninvasive technique (which, unlike ECT, does not require anesthesia, the induction of a seizure, or the associated memory loss) to see how efficacious it is in less refractory subjects.

THE NIMH IN THE ERA OF REINVENTING GOVERNMENT

Vignettes about my own and other younger Clinical Associates' experiences at the NIMH give a sense of the rich, unusual, and perhaps unique environment for academic and clinical research progress and innovation. They emphasize the critical importance of young trainees, not only for the acquisition of their career-training opportunities and mentoring, but for their reciprocal creativity and infusion of new ideas.

As a government agency, the NIH is vulnerable not only to trends in attitudes about (and thus funding of) clinical and basic science research, but also to politics and federal budgeting. The current atmosphere is one of mistrust of government, and the economic reality requires huge budget cuts to reduce the national deficit. The NIH Clinical Center, with some 500 beds, is currently slated for rebuilding at about half its size, with a projected 250-bed hospital. Clinical research, too, is under assault by the less costly, more flashy, exotic and promising, if not exaggerated, benefits of the molecular biology revolution.

With equal or greater budgetary, administrative, and fiscal problems in the extramural program of the NIMH, and the converging forces of Medicare funding cuts, managed care, and decreased grant funding and overhead recalculations, preservation of the clinical research programs of the Intramural Program appear to have even greater priority than ever before. The low percentage of funding of even excellent grant proposals in the extramural program has reduced that scientific enterprise to something of a lottery system, not necessarily fostering creativity and innovation over more conservative, "sure thing" types of projects. Increasingly, as money tightens and reviews multiply and become more "grantlike" in the Intramural Program, similar problems in the clinical research portfolio are likely to magnify.

In 25 years, however, and despite multiple academic or political disappointments, I have never regretted my decision to join and stay on at the NIMH. I have been privileged to work with many wonderful scientists and patients in an effort to understand better and to treat the serious, potentially life-threatening, recurrent psychiatric disorders.

The current neuroscience explosion has provided unparalleled opportunities for clinical advances in our understanding of the pathophysiology and treatment of the major psychiatric disorders. The Intramural Program has provided a rich and unique training ground and laboratory for the accomplishment of this enterprise. We look forward to its being strengthened in the future so that individual investigators can continue to make outstanding clinical and basic science contributions toward the better treatment of the common, yet too often devastating and lethal, psychiatric disorders of the central nervous system. A two- to three-year clinical or laboratory fellowship or a more extended NIMH career can be one of the most rewarding professional opportunities in medicine.

RECOMMENDED READING

Burke, J. D., Pincus, H. A. & Pardes, H. (1986), The clinician-researcher in psychiatry. *Amer. J. Psychiat.*, 143:968–975.

Goddard, G. V. (1969), A permanent change in brain function resulting from daily electrical stimulation. *Exp. Neurol.*, 25:295–230.

Haviland, M., Pincus, H. A., & Dial, T. (1987), Career, research involvement and research fellowship plans of potential psychiatrists. *Arch. Gen. Psychiat.*, 44:493–496.

Ketter, T. A., Andreason, P. J., George, M. S., Lee, C., Gill, D. S., Parekh, P. I., Willis, M. W., Herscovitch, P., & Post, R. M. (in press), Anterior paralimbic mediation of procaine-induced emotional and psychosensory experiences. *Arch. Gen. Psychiat.*

Morihisa, J. M. (1995), Zen and the art of biological psychiatry research. In: *Career Planning for Psychiatrists*, ed. K. M. Mohul & L. J. Dickstein. Washington, DC: American Psychiatric Press, pp. 17–24.

Post, R. M. (1975), Cocaine psychoses: A continuum model. *Amer. J. Psychiat.*, 132:225–231.

Post, R. M. (1992), Transduction of psychosocial stress into the neurobiology of recurrent affective disorder. *Amer. J . Psychiat.*, 149:999–1010.

Post, R. M. & Weiss, S. R. B. (1995), The neurobiology of treatment-resistant mood disorders. In: *Psychopharmacology: The Fourth Generation of Progress*, ed. F. E. Bloom & D. J. Kupfer. New York: Raven Press, pp. 1155–1170.

❊ 8 ❊

Academic-Turned-Administrator: The Psychiatrist-Executive

[ADMINISTRATION AND MANAGEMENT]

Arthur Lazarus

Dr. Lazarus is Medical Director of Northwestern Institute in Fort Washington, Pennsylvania, and Clinical Associate Professor of Psychiatry at Temple University School of Medicine, in Philadelphia. He was previously Medical Director and Physician Advisor for TAO/Green Spring Health Services, a managed behavioral health care organization providing patient-care services, precertification and concurrent review, and employee assistance programs. Dr. Lazarus is a nationally recognized teacher and expert in psychopharmacology, managed care, and behavioral health care administration. He has written over 75 articles and three books, including the soon-to-be-released*Controversies in Managed Mental Health Care*. Dr. Lazarus is a recipient of the Sigma Xi grant-in-aid of research award, the Upjohn Achievement Award for Excellence in Pharmacology, and the O. Spurgeon English Award for Excellence in Psychiatry. Dr. Lazarus is listed in *Who's Who in the East* and *Who's Who in Managed Health Care*. He is a member of the American College of Physician Executives, the College of Physicians of Philadelphia, and the Alpha Omega Alpha honor medical society.

A new type of health care expert is rapidly gaining credibility in medical circles: the psychiatrist-executive. Although it is not known how many psychiatrists are involved in administration, the American Medical Association has estimated that out of approximately 670,000 licensed physicians in the United States, nearly 15,000, or about 2% of physicians, devote most of their time to administration (Roback et al., 1994). According to a survey conducted by the Tampa-based Physician Executive Management Center among physician chief executive officers of hospitals, 38% are psychiatrists (Sherer, 1993).

One need only look at the membership figures of the American College of Physician Executives to find evidence of the growing number of physicians going into management. This organization, also located in Tampa, boasts a membership of over 9,000 physicians, about twice the number in 1990. Approximately 120 new members a month are swelling the ranks of the American College of Physician Executives (Mangan, 1993).

Psychiatrist-executives have sometimes been referred to as a new breed of physicians. They have been viewed as "fast-track" doctors because many have obtained graduate business degrees and have quickly progressed through the ranks of management. An article in *The Wall Street Journal* characterized physician-executives as persons who "can pivot quickly—at least in theory—between the world of stethoscopes and the world of spreadsheets" (Anders, 1994). While not all physician-executives are formally trained in business, most are management minded and capable of acting as liaisons between non-medical administrators and other physicians.

The role of the psychiatrist-executive has evolved rapidly in response to the health care crisis in the United States. In a study of 867 physician-executives, Kindig, Dunham, and Chun (1991) reported that typical physician managers entered their new career after 20 years in practice. Their primary objective was to ensure quality care and to have an impact on health care provision. Kindig et al. noted that 33.7% of these physician managers were working in hospitals, 21.8% in academic institutions, 21.2% in government agencies, and 23.3% in other organizations. Advancement to more senior-level executive positions appeared to require a willingness to move between organizations and across organizational types. These investigators speculated that the disproportionate number of older physician administrators in their study indicated that a shift of professional activities from clinical duties to managerial roles is becoming an increasingly common career move for physicians as they near retirement. Yet, increasingly, younger physicians are showing an interest in management and are seeking formal management training soon after residency training. The number of fellowships in administrative medicine is steadily increasing.

FINDING THE WAY

In *Demian*, Hermann Hesse comes to the conclusion that each person has but one genuine vocation—"to find the way to himself." Paradoxically, for most psychiatrists, this pathway is discovered mainly through the lives of other people—patients, mentors, and role models. My own career is no exception, and my interest in psychiatric administration developed gradually over many years. Several changes preceded my career in administration, which culminated in a decision to enter business school.

Academia

The academic phase of my career was relatively long, 12 years to be exact, from 1976 to 1988. It included the time I spent in medical school, trained in psychiatry, and remained on the active faculty of my medical school alma mater, Temple University. It was a period characterized primarily by research and writing about psychopharmacology and unusual psychiatric syndromes. I routinely taught residents and medical students. Many of the residents recognized my scholarly interests and nicknamed me "Article" Lazarus because I constantly cited the literature and wrote articles.

I can vividly recall several episodes during this period that affected me deeply, if for no other reason than that they remind me how important role models are for aspiring trainees. I recount them now because there are relatively few physicians who can counsel psychiatrists interested in management careers.

My first experience was as a senior medical student. I was struggling with the decision to become a psychiatrist or a neurologist. During a neurology rotation, I shared my quandary with a well-respected neurologist. Naturally, he advocated for his specialty. He said, "Art, if you want my opinion, one day psychiatry will become a subspecialty of neurology."

I repeated his comment to Charles Shagass, an internationally known psychiatrist on staff at Temple. Dr. Shagass told me that the neurologist was wrong, that one day psychiatry would become a subspecialty of toxicology! We both had a good laugh, and I realized that Dr. Shagass was someone I could confide in and count on for sage advice.

Later that year I studied under Dr. Shagass. He taught me electrophysiology and the essentials of writing research reports for scientific publication. Dr. Shagass was first and foremost a researcher and demonstrated that a psychiatrist doesn't have to see patients all his or her life. This dispelled a preconceived notion of mine that psychiatrists were basically people who practiced psychotherapy. Psychotherapy never interested me all that much, and I was relieved to hear Dr. Shagass say that research, not psychotherapy, was his first love and that he had become "bored" seeing patients.

Other well-known physicians have made similar comments. Robert Gumbiner (1994), chairman of the board of a large managed care organization, stated, "Nowadays, after completing residency a physician can do the same thing for 50 years. It gets boring after 10 or 15 years. Doctors are supposed to be teachers, planners, and organizers of care. They should serve more actively in some of these roles."

Another memorable experience occurred in the third year of my residency, during supervision with O. Spurgeon English, the founder of Temple University's Department of Psychiatry and a pioneer in psychosomatic medicine. I was jointly supervised with a fourth-year resident who had presented a very difficult case, that of a chronically depressed and suicidal, bulimic woman. In psychotherapy sessions, the resident was afraid to "push" the woman because he was fearful that she might attempt suicide. In fact, she had previously attempted suicide by jumping in front of a train. After hearing the case, Dr. English addressed the resident in the following manner: "The difference between you and me is that you're afraid of that damn train and I'm not!"

"Spurge" had an uncanny ability to size people up and take a position in relation to their problems. His therapy was a form of "tough love," and in this particular case he had determined that the patient would never prosper if left to her current defenses. His assessment led him to believe that the risk of intervening in a dramatic way outweighed the benefit of maintaining the status quo. He was also making a value judgment about the patient's life and openly acknowledging that psychotherapy could have detrimental effects.

Dr. English's remark about the train still haunts me today. At the time, it led to a lively discussion that touched on important issues that confront all clinicians today, such as ethics and the cost–quality relationship in health care. I have since come to realize that Spurge wanted to make psychotherapy as effective, inexpensive, and short as possible. He practiced managed care long before the term was coined.

In the final year of my residency I was elected Chief Resident. This was perhaps my first true management position, albeit part-time. I was fortunate to have been offered two jobs upon completing my residency. I was leaning toward staying at Temple, where I had been offered a junior faculty position working half-time on the inpatient unit and half-time on the consultation-liaison service. These areas of practice were always my favorite. The other position, running an outpatient diagnostic evaluation service at Belmont Center for Comprehensive Treatment (formerly Philadelphia Psychiatric Center), was intriguing but involved starting operations from scratch.

I was at a conference attended by the two psychiatrists who had made the offers – Anthony F. Panzetta, then Chairman of the Department of Psychiatry of Temple University, and Paul J. Fink, then Medical Director of Belmont Center. Dr. Panzetta literally held me by one arm while Dr. Fink held me by the other arm, each trying to claim me for their respective positions. Needless to say, it was very flattering to have two prominent psychiatrists vying for my talents. I decided to stay at Temple because I was comfortable there and I relished the academic environment. Ironically, I left Temple four years later for a position at Belmont Center very similar to the one that Dr. Fink had originally offered me.

Pseudoacademia

The next three years, 1988 to 1991, I directed an inpatient diagnostic evaluation unit at Belmont Center for Comprehensive Treatment. This position attracted me for several reasons.

First, going to Belmont Center gave me an opportunity to work with Dr. Fink, a leading figure in American psychiatry. Second, my salary increased significantly (nobody claimed that academia paid well). Third, the unit was designed to be short term, in anticipation of the penetration of managed care companies in Philadelphia. Fourth, the position combined the best of academia and private practice.

There was nothing "false" about this position. I considered it "pseudoacademia" only in the sense that, for the first time in my career, I was permanently, physically separated from a medical school campus. In retrospect, cutting the apron strings was necessary. Dealing with the separation anxiety at this time helped make future transitions easier and eliminated any second-guessing that would have been associated with a one-track career.

My three years at Belmont Center were rewarding and productive. I especially cherished the relationships I made with the medical staff— relationships that I maintain today. I was, however, becoming less interested in rendering direct patient care and supervising medical students and residents on a daily basis. Dr. Fink recognized this and called me into his office one day. We had a long talk, and he suggested that maybe it was time to reconsider my career goals and interests. No one until then, except for my analyst, had had such a candid conversation with me about my career.

Shortly after our talk, I decided to leave Belmont Center and become the Medical Director of a growing managed care organization where I had been working part-time for many years. Dr. Fink's parting words were, "I'm sorry to see you go, Art, but at least they're getting a good medical director."

Managed Care

I left Belmont Center in 1991 and assumed a full-time position as the Medical Director of Bustleton Health Systems, Inc., a large behavioral group practice that had contracts to provide mental health and substance abuse services for HMO patients. At this stage in my career, I was clearly more interested in *systems* of treatment rather than treatment per se. Only 25% of my time was now spent in direct patient care. In the remaining time, I did utilization review and participated in quality assurance, risk-management, credentialing, and other activities.

By a strange twist of events, I was soon reunited with my former mentor, Anthony F. Panzetta. Dr. Panzetta had left Temple in 1985 and founded TAO, Inc., a psychiatric utilization review organization operating under the auspices of Independence Blue Cross (formerly Blue Cross of Philadelphia). TAO was expanding and purchased Bustleton Health Systems in 1992, six months after I had become their Medical Director. Simultaneously, I became Medical Director of TAO's provider network, essentially continuing the same line of work I had done at Bustleton.

The merger between TAO and Bustleton positioned me in a different venue, namely, a midsize corporation. It was very sobering to be outnumbered by lay administrators, some of whom ranked above me in the organization. Indeed, the very existence of an organizational hierarchy and explicit lines of reporting was new to me, and I had to adjust to corporate life. I determined to narrow the communication gap between physicians and nonphysician managers. Many physician-executives have testified that bridging this gap is the single greatest challenge they face in the course of their work.

In 1994, TAO merged with a larger behavioral managed care organization, Green Spring Health Services, Inc., headquartered in Columbia, Maryland. This merger occurred at a time when the pace of health care acquisitions was brisk, as it is today. The merger between TAO and Green Spring piqued my interest in administration and managed care delivery systems. Yet, I had advanced as far in the company as I could, given that the new corporate headquarters were over 100 miles away and my role was limited primarily to that of a physician advisor (peer reviewer).

Less than a year after the merger, I jumped at the opportunity to become the medical director of a local psychiatric hospital that was part of an integrated delivery system and on the verge of expanding. In conversations with hospital executives before I was actually hired, I proposed moving toward a staff model with full-time, salaried psychiatrists (i.e., a "mini" department of psychiatry), implementing an incentive plan to reward psychiatrists for cost-effective treatment (e.g., short lengths of stay without recidivism), converting specialty units to acute care units, and eliminating inefficiencies in treatment by tightening links between hospital, partial hospital, and outpatient treatment programs. My goal was to ensure that patients were transitioned appropriately through the treatment continuum and that physicians were following patients through the continuum whenever possible. This position has provided more depth than any position I have ever held.

OBTAINING AN M.B.A. DEGREE

I matriculated in business school in August, 1994, while I was still working at TAO (I will graduate in July, 1996). There is a wide range of opinion whether it is advisable for management-oriented physicians to acquire a business degree. The consensus seems to be that the more serious one is about administration and leaving practice to devote full-time effort to management, the more important it is to have a graduate business degree. If nothing else, an M.B.A. adds value to one's vita and enhances a physician's marketability.

A recent survey by Whit/Kieffer, Ford, Hadelman, and Lloyd, an Oak Brook, Illinois, recruiting firm, found that 9.4% of physicians in management positions had M.B.A.s, an increase of 6% from 1990 (Lloyd and Lyons, 1995). Moreover, another 38% of physicians in the survey said that they were working on an M.B.A. or intended to pursue one. Other surveys, however, have found that the time and energy needed to pursue an advanced management degree is simply too great a burden for busy physicians.

My solution to overcoming the time pressure was to enroll in an "executive" M.B.A. program. Executive M.B.A. programs differ from traditional M.B.A. programs in many respects. They are usually given on weekends (my courses were given on alternating Fridays and Saturdays) and take only two years to complete. Executive M.B.A. programs do not require "foundation" courses as do most traditional M.B.A. programs. In a sense, experience counts for credit in executive M.B.A. programs. Students usually have a minimum of five to ten years of work experience prior to entering the program. The average age of students in my class at the time of admission was 37.

An executive M.B.A. program comes as close as any graduate program to providing physicians the necessary skills to manage the "medical-industrial complex." Typical courses include accounting, statistics, economics, finance, marketing, business law and ethics, strategic management, operations management, management information systems, and human resource administration. Because instruction occurs primarily on Fridays and Saturdays, executive M.B.A. programs interfere minimally with employment and practice. On the other hand, owing to the accelerated pace and amount of work assigned, students must spend an additional 10 to 20 hours per week studying outside the classroom.

For many physicians, there is an "opportunity" cost to attend an executive M.B.A. program, namely, the loss of some earnings while one is in school for two years. Moreover, tuition is expensive, ranging from less than $20,000 to more that $60,000 for both years. But the expected professional "payback" for M.B.A. degree holders is quite high (Weeks et al., 1994). Physician Executive Management Center estimates that physicians with management degrees earn about 7% more than those without them (Mangan, 1993). Also, many companies reimburse students part of the tuition or all of it.

There are many other types of programs and advanced degrees available to psychiatrists interested in medical management. Most of these programs are less intensive than executive M.B.A. programs, and some may actually be more beneficial because they provide specific instruction in health care administration, whereas executive M.B.A. programs rarely offer electives or provide specialization in health care. The important point is that for psychiatrists who want to pursue a career in administration, it is almost imperative for them to seek additional training beyond residency. The old method by which many physicians acquired management skills – through experience and by trial and error – is no longer adequate in a competitive business environment.

THE CLINICAL CHALLENGE

That my career evolved slowly from academia seems to be typical of many physician-executives. What is perhaps not so typical is that I have stopped seeing outpatients. Initially, this became necessary once I entered business school. But my decision to cut down on practicing also came naturally, as a result of losing interest in treating patients. Other physicians who have become administrators have commented that they too became uninterested in one-on-one patient care, preferring instead to manage populations rather than individuals. Some physicians found that practicing and managing were incompatible due to the different demands of each activity. Conceptually, it may make more sense to focus on skills training for psychiatric administrators and concentrate on practice essentials for clinicians.

There are skeptics who can't imagine blending business and psychiatry or replacing a clinical career with a nonclinical one. I was actually told by a hospital administrator (not a physician) to maintain a private practice, if only to maintain credibility among my peers. But who are my peers? Other psychiatrists? Nonphysician managers? The answer, of course, is both, since ultimately psychiatrist-executives lead a double existence and identify with physicians *and* administrators. Again, this speaks to the value of business training for psychiatrists. They must be able to speak the same language as administrators.

The other side of the coin, maintaining one's clinical acumen, is equally important. In my opinion, however, treating patients is not the only way to keep abreast of the latest clinical developments and show your colleagues that you haven't "joined the suits." Psychiatric administrators can take advantage of any number of continuing medical education courses to stay clinically sharp. My credo is that you can take the administrator out of academia, but you shouldn't be able to take academia out of the administrator.

CONCLUSION

My advice to young psychiatrists entertaining the notion of becoming administrators is the same as the advice I gave them when I taught psychopharmacology: start low and go slow. Before considering any type of graduate training in business administration, attend seminars and workshops to see if you are attracted to the management field. Excellent programs are offered by the American Psychiatric Association, the American Association of Child and Adolescent Psychiatry, the American Medical Associaton, the American College of Physician Executives, the Institute for Behavioral Healthcare, and the American Managed Care and Review Association.

Volunteer, if possible, for assignments that involve administrative or leadership expertise, such as chairing committees or leading teams of people. Don't worry if you think you are not a "born leader" or do not have the "right" personality or temperament to be a leader. The truth is that effective leadership is really associated with competence in one's role, not personality style.

You must advocate for yourself and vigorously pursue all reasonable opportunities in management. I campaigned for chief resident and sold Dr. Fink on the idea of a managed care unit by submitting a written proposal to him. I wrote a similar proposal for my most recent job. I continue to publish articles and books to demonstrate expertise in my field and promote myself. Although the health care scene is rapidly changing, *you* contol your destiny and hold the key to new horizons. Don't depend on others to make things happen for you.

Psychiatrist-executives, if properly trained, should be able to work in many different types of organizations and health care systems. Top level psychiatrist-executives should be able to navigate between the worlds of medicine and of management and between various medical disciplines. Several psychiatrists have risen to the rank of dean of medical schools and chief executive officer of large corporations. These psychiatrists have a bright future because the field of health care is constantly changing and their input is vital to the reconfiguration of medical delivery systems. I enthusiastically recommend the management field to psychiatrists who would like to participate in this change and help shape the future of a noble profession.

REFERENCES AND RECOMMENDED READING

Anders, G. (1994), A new breed of M.D.s add M.B.A. to vita. *Wall Street Journal*, September 27, pp. B1, B10

Curry, W., ed. (1988), *Roads to Medical Management: Physician Executives' Career Decisions.* Tampa, FL: American Academy of Medical Directors.

Gumbiner, R. (1994), Perspectives of an HMO leader. *Inquiry*, 31:330–333.

Hodge, R. H. Jr. & Nash, D. B. (1993), The physician-executive. In: *Future Practice Alternatives in Medicine, 2nd ed.*, ed. D. Nash. New York: Igaku-Shoin, pp. 237–266.

Kindig, D. A., Dunham, N. C., & Chun, L.M. (1991), Career paths of physician executives. *Health Care Manage. Rev.*, 16(4):11–20.

Lazarus, A. (1995), From stethoscope to spreadsheet: The physician with an M.B.A. *The Pharos*, 58(2):20–23.

Lazarus, A. (1995), The psychiatrist-executive revisited: New role, new economics. *Psychiatr. Ann.*, 25:494–499.

Lloyd, J. S. & Lyons, M. F. (1995), The physician executive "arrives"— A new generation prepares for the future. *Physician Exec.*, 8:22–26.

Mangan, D. (1993), Lured by the promise of a new career: Read this first. *Med. Econom.*, November 22, pp. 159–169.

Roback, G., Randolph, L., Seidman, B., & Pasko, T. (1994), *Physician Characteristics and Distribution in the U.S.* Chicago: American Medical Association.

Sherer, J. L. (1993), Physician CEOs: Ranks continue to grow. *Hospitals*, 67(9):42.

Walsh, D. C. (1987), *Corporate Physicians: Between Medicine and Management.* New Haven, CT: Yale University Press.

Weeks, W. B., Wallace, A. E., Wallace, M. M., et al. (1994), A comparison of the educational costs and incomes of physicians and other professionals. *N. Eng. J. Med.*, 330:1280–1286.

❈ 9 ❈

The Other Half of the Equation: A Psychiatrist in the Workplace

[OCCUPATIONAL PSYCHIATRY]

Len Sperry

Dr. Sperry is a Professor in the Department of Psychiatry and Behavioral Medicine and in the Department of Preventive Medicine at the Medical College of Wisconsin, where he is also Director of its Division of Organizational Psychiatry and Corporate Health and coordinates a fellowship program in Organizational Psychiatry. He is a member of the Committee on Occupational Psychiatry of the American Psychiatric Association, a member of the Committee of Occupational Psychiatry of the Group for the Advancement of Psychiatry (GAP), and is currently vice-president of the Academy of Organizational and Occupational Psychiatry. He has published over 200 articles in professional journals, including many about the practice of organizational and occupational psychiatry, as well as 20 books including *Psychiatric Consultation in the Workplace* and the forthcoming volume: *Corporate Consultation and Therapy*. Dr. Sperry is on the editorial boards of nine journals. He is board certified in both psychiatry and clinical psychology and is a fellow of the American Psychological Association and the American Psychiatric Association.

Let's begin with an increasingly common case presentation: I saw Jason L. on referral from his company's EAP. He is a 48-year-old regional manager who presented with depression, insomnia, general malaise, and chronic worry. He has been with his company for 18 years and quickly rose through the ranks to his present position. To remain competitive, the company has been going through a series of downsizings for the past two years. One of the most difficult parts of Jason's job has been laying off or discharging sales reps and office staff who have become close friends. He finds this task increasingly difficult and painful and doesn't think he can continue doing it. He describes laying awake nights ruminating about his laid-off friends: Have they found jobs yet? Are they angry with him? Can he face the prospects of discharging any more of the people who report to him? Jason reports that his personal life has been going as well as ever. He notes he is happily married and recently celebrated his 25th wedding anniversary with a surprise trip to Honolulu which was arranged by their three grown children. In short, Jason voices no complaints about his life outside his job, except that recently he has had little interest and energy in partaking of it.

How might a psychiatrist formulate this case, and what are the most appropriate interventions? The usual and customary way of formulating cases—at least from a psychodynamic perspective—is to search for an intrapsychic or interpersonal conflict regarding the domain of love. But the issue here does not involve Jason's love life; it involves his work life. And what about intervention? Should it be medication? Conventional psychotherapy? Work-focused psychotherapy? Or should it be executive coaching or an organizational intervention?

The ability to love and the ability to work are believed to be the two essential criteria for mental health. Unfortunately, psychiatric practice rarely reflects this belief. For all practical purposes, psychiatry has emphasized the love dimension of the love-work-mental health equation with almost no regard for the work domain. Nonetheless, the link between work and mental health is unequivocal, and research suggests that work may be more basic to self-esteem than is love or friendship (Vaillant, 1979; Savickas, 1990). Work clearly affects not only one's personal identity, but also one's family and health status (Vaillant and Vaillant, 1981). Unfortunately, psychiatry residents have little if any training or experience with the work domain, that is, the value and meaning of work and its impact on psychological functioning, and the importance of taking a complete work history and incorporating this information into the treatment plan. In a national survey of residency directors (Sperry, 1995), I found that three-fourths of residencies have no formal training in the psychiatric aspects of work.

WORKPLACE PSYCHIATRY DEFINED

What is workplace psychiatry, and what do psychiatric consultants in the workplace do? Let's begin with a brief description and history of the subspecialty. Workplace psychiatry—also called industrial, occupational, organizational, or corporate psychiatry—emphasizes the relationship of work to physical and mental health and well-being. Workplace psychiatrists study the psychopathology that individuals bring to the work setting and the psychopathology that results from it, as well as factors that promote healthy behaviors and functioning.

A 1917 article by Adler on psychiatric symptoms in jobless men probably represents the first publication in workplace psychiatry. The first book on industrial psychiatry was published in 1929 (Anderson, 1929), and the first "Review of Industrial Psychiatry" appeared in the *American Journal of Psychiatry* in April 1927 (Sherman, 1927). Following that auspicious beginning, the stature of workplace psychiatry has alternatively risen and fallen. Psychiatrists were the dominant force in occupational psychiatry and mental health until the early 1980s, when nonmedical professionals moved into the field with the proliferation of employee assistance programs (EAPs).

Workplace psychiatry has recently been "rediscovered" with the reestablishment of the APA Committee on Occupational Psychiatry in 1986. Furthermore, the Academy of Organizational and Occupational Psychiatry (AOOP) began in 1990, and the mission of the GAP Committee on Psychiatry in Industry was updated and the committee renamed the Committee on Occupational Psychiatry in early 1993. Memberships in AOOP have increased geometrically in the past several years. Membership includes psychiatrists experienced as internal or external consultants to corporations, managed care organizations, universities, government, and the military, as well as psychiatrists who are looking for an alternative to traditional clinical practice or an alternative to the direction health care appears to be taking. The demand for quality psychiatric consultative and clinical services to work organizations primarily accounts for these developments. AOOP was established, in large part, to provide access to various educational and training opportunities, as well as to develop a referral network. Finally, an increasing literature on various aspects of workplace psychiatry have been published in the past few years. Two books, *Psychiatric Consultation in the Workplace* (Sperry, 1993), *Mental Health in the Workplace* (Kahn, 1993), and the very practical monograph, *Introduction to Occupational Psychiatry* (Comittee on Occupational Psychiatry, 1994), are notable.

AREAS OF WORKPLACE PSYCHIATRIC PRACTICE

There are three main areas of practice in workplace psychiatry: direct clinical services, consultation, and applied research.

Direct Clinical Services

A variety of direct clinical workplace psychiatric services can be competently provided by most general psychiatrists. These services include psychiatric disability evaluation, medication evaluation and monitoring, and other psychiatric interventions to hourly employees and management. Referral is often made by the corporate medical director or by EAP personnel. These clinical services may be provided on site or in the psychiatrist's office. Since corporate executives are unlikely to utilize their firm's EAP, they are usually referred to outside psychiatrists for individual psychotherapy, couples therapy, psychiatric evaluation, or medication evaluation and management.

Consultation

Perhaps the most common form of consultation with employees is case management. The occupational psychiatrist evaluates the employee, plans and coordinates appropriate treatment and referral if necessary, and sees to it that necessary information about the employee's health and work status is conveyed to appropriate parties. Periodically, the psychiatrist reviews progress and follows up as necessary. A more specialized area of consultation involves work disability and competency to work/fitness for work evaluations.

A developing area of workplace psychiatric consultation involves work with executives. The psychiatrist may be asked to evaluate a candidate for an executive position; advise a CEO or vice-president on motivating, promoting, or firing a staff member; or serve as a sounding board, advisor, or medical expert on professional concerns of an executive. The psychiatrist may also be engaged to provide or arrange for an executive seminar on any number of mental health and work topics.

As business increasingly embraces the concept of work teams, occupational psychiatrists are being called on to work with project and management teams to increase their effectiveness through team building, conflict-resolution, communications training, and programs to enhance cultural diversity in the workplace. Occupational psychiatrists are also being engaged to assist with organization-wide issues, such as diagnosing complex organizational problems, modifying corporate culture, developing integrated corporate mental health policies, and reviewing corporate mental health benefits.

Applied Research

The workplace provides numerous opportunities for doing applied research on factors affecting employee health and well-being as well as dysfunction. Areas of applied research include epidemiological studies of psychopathology and stress-related disorders and conditions and their determinants; developing integrated health and mental health care tracking systems to ensure continuity and quality of care; and initiating surveillance systems to track highly vulnerable individuals and stressful areas of the corporation.

PSYCHIATRISTS VERSUS PSYCHOLOGISTS AS WORKPLACE CONSULTANTS

I'm often asked if there's really any difference between psychiatrists and psychologists who consult to work organizations and if psychiatrists make any unique contribution to work-related issues. There are two types of psychologists with a workplace orientation: industrial/organizational psychologists (I/O) and organizational psychologists (O/P).

Industrial/organizational psychologists typically work with adults within the normal range of psychological functioning to enhance human performance and the quality of life within work organizations.

Their primary functions within organizations are employee selection, establishing assessment centers, conducting performance appraisal test validation and attitude surveys, and teaching and research. Coursework in an I/O program typically includes work motivation theory, personnel selection methods, performance appraisal and feedback, human factors engineering, career development, decision theory, program evaluation, and research methods. I/O programs follow the so-called scientist/practitioner model of training. Finally, becoming licensed or certified as a psychologist is not required of I/O psychologists in many states. Essentially, I/O psychologists are not trained or licensed to provide therapeutic interventions for people with psychiatric disturbances or disorders.

There is a subset of I/O psychologists who identify themselves as organizational psychologists (O/P). They tend to focus on organizational diagnosis and development efforts and are more likely to have degrees in organizational psychology, organizational development, or organizational behavior. Unlike I/O programs, these programs follow the so-called scholar/practitioner model of training and emphasize psychosocial factors. Their goal is to train organizational practitioners rather than I/O specialists. Coursework includes organizational theory, organizational culture, organizational behavior, organizational assessment, and consultation strategies. Supervised on-site internship training in organizational development activities in the internal or external consultant role is also required.

Neither the I/O nor the O/P program prepares students for clinical intervention, thus limiting such psychologists' involvement with psychiatric presentations in the workplace. For this reason, some graduate programs offer joint or dual training in clinical psychology and I/O psychology for which licensure to practice clinical psychology is possible.

It is here that I believe psychiatrists have the most to offer as workplace consultants. Because of their medical and clinical psychiatry training and experience, psychiatrists are well suited to deal with clinical and crisis issues in the workplace. The biopsychosocial and medical models that underlie psychiatric training are quite distinct from the "scientist-professional" or "scholar-practitioner" models of training for organizational psychologists. Furthermore, the clientele of workplace psychiatrists is much broader than that for psychologists in that normal functioning as well as clinically symptomatic workers, teams, and whole organizations are consulted with. The range of specific interventions of workplace psychiatrists is quite broad and includes disability and fitness-for-duty evaluations, playing a role in determining mental health policy, benefits consultation, executive coaching, consulting, and psychotherapy, and crisis-intervention/stress debriefing.

EXPERIENCE AS A WORKPLACE CONSULTANT

I remember my introduction to workplace psychology/psychiatry well. I was a graduate student in psychology taking a course dealing with work and disability. I needed to add one more course to be a full-time student, and it was the only one that fit my schedule. Needless to say, going into the course, I had little interest in the subject matter. The lectures were uninspiring, but I found the readings fascinating. As my graduate work continued, I pursued other courses in organizations and organizational behavior and took seminars in group process and group therapy. During this time I became involved with two large-scale planned change projects where I had the opportunity to function as a change agent or consultant. I found these projects to be both enormously challenging and satisfying.

My doctoral dissertation involved the effects of different leadership styles and expectations on work team functioning. After graduation, I began a full-time academic career doing university teaching and also started consulting work organizations on a part-time basis. I taught a consultation course as well as other courses that involved organizational behavior topics. My consulting activities involved both executive assessments and executive consulting and coaching. When the opportunity arose to plan and implement a leadership and management development program for all the middle and top managers of a multinational corporation with 10 subsidiaries, I jumped at the chance. Over the course of four years, I headed up a team of inside and outside consultants and trained 120 senior managers. I quickly learned that such organizational consultation involved considerable travel and time away from my family. During this time I also started doing disability evaluations.

I had started college as a premed major and quickly shifted to psychology. My interest and aptitude for science and medicine, however, had not waned. After seven years of teaching and consulting, I decided to complete my premed requirements and apply to medical school. My desire was to combine psychiatry and preventive medicine — with an emphasis on health promotion — and I was pleased when the Medical College of Wisconsin offered me the opportunity to complete residencies in both fields simultaneously. Interestingly, the preventive medicine program required coursework in administration and management. Thereafter, a fellowship in Behavioral Medicine at the University of Wisconsin Medical School allowed me to learn additional coaching and consultation skills, which proved useful in working with the health concerns of executives.

After completing the residencies and fellowship, I was offered a faculty position in both psychiatry and preventive medicine at the Medical College of Wisconsin. In addition to serving as Medical Director for the outpatient psychiatry clinic, which trained our psychiatry residents, I was able to develop and teach seminars for senior residents and faculty on organizational diagnosis, psychodynamics of organizations, and work-focused psychotherapy. In time, a senior rotation and a fellowship in organizational psychiatry developed in the Department of Psychiatry. At about the same time, I was asked to plan and implement a course on industrial and organizational psychology for the master's in public health (MPH) program in occupational medicine in the Department of Preventive Medicine. This course is now in its sixth year. Recently, I was asked to develop an additional course for the MPH program which was titled: Organizational Behavior and Design. I have also been involved in a research project for the college's Foley Center for Aging and Development. We have just completed a project studying the physical, psychological, and relational changes in senior executives in the two years following retirement. I particularly enjoy the mix of teaching, research, and consultation. As I could not earlier, when I maintained full-time consultation practice, which required considerable travel, I now pick and choose from among the consultation requests I receive those which are both interesting and close to home.

My consultation experiences since completing medical school, residency, and fellowship continue to include executive consultation and coaching, as well as consultation with work teams. I employ my medical training regularly in my consultation with senior executives. As a psychologist doing organizational and executive consultation, I was limited in responding to the health concerns of a distressed executive with whom I consulted. Currently, a number of my consultations include members of the board of directors of nonprofit corporations and involve consultation interventions ranging from strategic planning to intergroup conflict resolution to modifying the culture of a given organization. In the past three years there has been considerably more call for the clinical or crisis-related type of consulting I have come to call "corporate consulting and therapy." This includes organizations in the throes of major changes such as downsizing or merging, or executives in crisis, or the occasional situation in which both the corporation and one or more of its executives are in crisis simultaneously. It is in such clinical or crisis-oriented situations that I believe that organizational psychiatrists are the consultants of choice.

GETTING INVOLVED IN WORKPLACE PSYCHIATRY

Becoming a psychiatric consultant in the workplace involves a socialization process by which the psychiatrist begins to think and act like a consultant and is able to adapt to and find acceptance in the workplace environment. This is not to suggest that the psychiatrist relinquishes his or her identity as a physician or psychiatrist; rather, the psychiatrist extends his or her role and repertoire of knowledge and skills to include both its consultative and its clinical dimensions. In other words, a psychiatrist who practices full-time in a workplace context functions as a consultant while retaining clinical acumen, whereas a psychiatrist who is sensitive to workplace issues and who practices in a clinical context functions as a clinician with organizational acumen.

The increasing complexity of work organizations and psychiatric issues involving workers requires that those who aspire to function as psychiatric consultants in the workplace have considerable knowledge and skill in organizational dynamics, organizational diagnosis, and organizational interventions. There is relatively little training in workplace consultation in psychiatry residency or fellowship programs at present (Sperry, 1995). In the past most workplace psychiatrists acquired a knowledge base and skills through actual experience and had little opportunity for training, reflection, or supervision.

A recent Group for the Advancement of Psychiatry (Committee on Occupational Psychiatry, 1994) report describes the career paths of eight well-regarded workplace psychiatrists. The ways in which each entered this subspecialty, developed a working knowledge and skills, and established a reputation makes for interesting reading and spells out a number of possibilities for practice in this field. Given the range of conceptual knowledge and skills that must be acquired, translated, extended, or unlearned if one is to function effectively in the workplace, it is not unreasonable to suggest that a psychiatrist seek formal opportunities to learn about and reflect on the transition from clinician to consultant. But what formal opportunities are available? Summer training institutes are offered, such as the ones held at Cape Cod, Massachusetts, with well-known organizational psychologists like Harry Levinson and Edgar Schein. Week-long seminars and workshops on organizational diagnosis, organizational dynamics, changing corporate culture, and the like are also offered.

The most common and accessible training opportunities, however are found in graduate schools of business administration or management. Along with credit courses in such areas as organizational behavior, human resources management, organization development, and management consultation, these schools offer noncredit courses and seminars on these and related topics. A number of graduate programs in psychology also offer coursework in industrial and organizational psychology. Some graduate public health programs offer similar management coursework and training that is attractive to some psychiatrists because of public health's close affiliation with medicine.

It is becoming increasingly common for psychiatrists who are interested in administrative psychiatry or other areas of medical management to enroll in M.B.A. programs. The American College of Physician Executives (ACPE) offers board certification to physicians who function in executive capacities. Although ACPE does not require an M.B.A. or similar graduate degree, it requires the equivalent of formal coursework. Currently, the American Board of Medical Specialties is considering a specialty in medical management. If it is approved, a physician seeking certification would need a graduate degree in management, among other requirements. It seems to me that a graduate degree in administration, management, human resources management, or, especially, organizational psychology, organizational behavior or organizational development will become a minimal expectation for those who plan to function as psychiatric consultants in the workplace. Currently, some M.B.A. programs offer specific coursework in the consultation process. So do a number of graduate programs in organizational psychology. This training can be helpful, but it is not sufficient for competent and ethical practice in certain areas of workplace psychiatry, such as organization-wide interventions.

Currently, there is no specific degree program for workplace psychiatry. Thus, even with formal graduate training in a related specialty of management or administration, an aspiring workplace psychiatrist will need to find specific training and experience to become socialized to think and act like a workplace psychiatrist. This can probably be arranged through a supervised apprenticeship with an experienced workplace psychiatrist or through a "miniresidency." It may be possible to arrange a miniresidency in workplace psychiatry with a senior member in the field. Such a training experience might involve spending four or more weeks on site in a training capacity with an individual or a group of workplace psychiatrists. Other forms of supervised training might be arranged, such as supervision of ongoing consultations with an experienced workplace psychiatrist. Ideally, this would involve face-to-face meetings, but it could also occur in regular telephone conferences if distance is a factor.

Recently, the APA Committee on Occupational Psychiatry began sponsoring useful courses and a workshop on the practice of workplace psychiatry at the APA annual meeting. The AOOP has also sponsored short courses and programs at the annual APA meeting and weekend workshops with CME credit at its own annual meetings in January.

Finally, some psychiatry residency and occupational medicine residency programs provide elective training, supervision, or both. The well-regarded industrial and occupational psychiatry program at Cornell University has trained approximately 60 psychiatrists over the years, many of whom have clinical appointments at various medical schools. Since 1993, a year-long fellowship in occupational and organizational psychiatry has been sponsored by the Department of Psychiatry and Mental Health Sciences at the Medical College of Wisconsin in Milwaukee. Senior electives in workplace psychiatry have also been offered.

There is a difference, as noted earlier, between knowledge and skills acquired through experience without time to reflect or to be supervised, and experience-based learning that has these components. At least one ethicist (Lowman, 1993) has questioned whether a clinical psychologist can hold himself or herself out as an organizational consultant without prior formal training or expertise and not violate the ethical standard of the American Psychological Association. Whether there is a similar ethical concern for psychiatrists is a consideration for the American Psychiatric Association. The issue of competence to practice workplace psychiatry remains a serious professional issue.

When can a psychiatrist claim that he or she has sufficient training and expertise to practice workplace psychiatry competently and ethically? My opinion is that minimal preparation for workplace psychiatric consultation involves a graduate degree in a relevant management discipline, a basic reading knowledge of the field, and some period of supervised experience.

CONCLUSION

Workplace psychiatry was one of the first areas of psychiatric practice to develop at the beginning of this century. It has only recently been rediscovered and will help the field of psychiatry remain a viable and growing specialty. Workplace psychiatry will continue to provide psychiatrists an alternative to the traditional practice of clinical psychiatry. At a time when the philosophy and economies of managed care seem to be too bitter a pill for our ailing health care system, workplace consultation has much to offer psychiatrists willing to broaden and translate their training and experience. Certainly workplace psychiatry has made, and will continue to make, an enduring contribution to the field and to humankind by articulating the other half of the equation.

REFERENCES

Adler, H. (1917), Unemployment and personality. *Mental Hygiene*, 1:16–24.

Anderson, V. (1929), *Psychiatry in Industry*. New York: Harper & Brothers.

Committee on Occupational Psychiatry Group for the Advancement of Psychiatry (1994), *Introduction to Occupational Psychiatry*, Report No.138. Washington, DC: American Psychiatric Press.

Kahn, J. (1993), *Mental Health in the Workplace: A Practical Psychiatric Guide*. New York: Van Nostrand Reinhold.

Lowman, R. (1993), *Counseling and Psychotherapy of Work Dysfunctions*. Washington, DC: American Psychological Association Books.

Savickas, M. (1990), Work and adjustment. In: *Behavior and Medicine*, ed. D. Wedding. St. Louis, MO: Mosby.

Sherman,M. (1927), A review of industrial psychiatry. *Amer. J. Psychiat.*, 83:701–710.

Sperry, L., ed. (1993), *Psychiatric Consultation in the Workplace*. Washington, DC: American Psychiatric Press.

Sperry, L. (1995), Residency education, work-related issues and organizational and occupational psychiatry. *Acad. Psychiat.*, 19:44–45.

Vaillant, G. (1979), Natural history of male psychological health: Effects of mental health on physical health. *New Eng. J. Med.*, 301:1249–1254.

Vaillant, G. & Vaillant, C. (1981), Natural history of male psychological health—X: Work as a predictor of positive mental health. *Amer. J. Psychiat.*, 138:1433–1440.

10

Defensive Medicine: A Career in the Air Force

[MILITARY PSYCHIATRY]

M. Richard Fragala

Dr. Fragala was the Chief Consultant for Psychiatry and Mental Health to the Air Force Surgeon General. In this capacity he was responsible for the management of the approximately 120 Air Force psychiatrists stationed all over the world, and for the residency training programs in psychiatry that the Air Force operates. He also was responsible for Air Force psychiatry and mental health policy and programs, which includes interfacing with the Department of Defense, the United States Congress, and various intelligence agencies. He was, in addition, the Chief, Division of Mental Health, at the Air Force Medical Center at Andrews Air Force Base, Maryland, where he was responsible for the Departments of Psychiatry, Psychology, Social Work, and Mental Health Nursing, which include inpatient adult (50 beds), substance abuse (25 beds), consultation-liason, and two outpatient clinic services. Dr. Fragala is Professor of Clinical Psychiatry at the Uniformed Services School of Medicine and is a Teaching Analyst at the Washington Psychoanalytic Institute. He is currently Superintendent, Clifton T. Perkins Hospital Center in Jessup, Maryland.

I was a most unlikely career military person, but having received a draft notice at the beginning of my senior year of medical school in 1968, I thought I would make some inquiry as to the training options available. I learned that if I opted for the Air Force at that time, I would be assured an internship at that service's 700-bed Wilford Hall Medical Center in San Antonio, along with an opportunity to compete to remain for residency training thereafter. At the height of the Vietnam War, the possibility of being able actually to complete a

113

Ipsychiatry residency directly out of internship seemed remote at best, but at least this way there was a chance.

I walked around with the papers for a few weeks, and then I ended up as the target of a sniper in the snack bar of an inner-city hospital. I was saved by a policeman who tackled me just in time. I signed the contract on the very next day, and when I tell the story of my enlistment, I always add that I joined the military to get out of the war!

I was able to complete residency training, and was assigned, as I'd requested, to the hospital at Andrews Air Force Base. Six months later, the prisoners of war were released from North Vietnam. The opportunity to work with this group of individuals, some of whom had been held captive for up to seven years, was an extraordinary experience, for which I remain very grateful. After only nine months, however, the person who occupied my current position as consultant called me one day and asked, "Do you like Chinese food?" I thought he was going to invite me to dinner. When I said I did, he replied, "That's really good, because you're going to be living on Taiwan in six weeks."

And so I was. I lived in Taichung in central Taiwan, where the State Department operated a Chinese-language school. I got to do clinical and commander consultations all over Southeast Asia. The American Psychiatric Association made me a District Branch (you had to belong to one to remain a member), and the American Board of Psychiatry and Neurology sent to the Philippines the written board examination, which I took with some Navy and Army colleagues.

When I returned to the States, I planned to take the oral boards, complete my service obligation, and begin psychoanalytic training. I had a separation date arranged but was approached by the consultant once again. I was prepared this time for the ethnic food ruse, but instead he offered a sponsored fellowship for my analytic training.

I remained in Washington for all six years and then for the additional two that it took to become certified by the American Psychoanalytic Association. I was then sent back to San Antonio to chair the program where I had been a resident.

Thereafter I returned to Washington, first as a faculty member at the Uniformed Services School of Medicine, and was then assigned to the Surgeon General's office as the Consultant for Psychiatry. After a year's orientation, I returned to the hospital at Andrews in my current clinical/administrative role while maintaining responsibility for the personnel, policy, and program elements for all Air Force mental health.

This career overview does not quite capture the four years I spent as an inpatient ward attending while seeing four control cases; the no-notice deployments to unknown locations (that is until you get there) for unknown periods; the field exercises, which included the need to acquire camping skills (bring a cellular phone, Domino's really does deliver!); the clinical and administrative problems surrounding the management of newly released hostages; the interaction with congressional staffers and members; JCAHO Surveyor Training; Flight Surgeon Training; and the countless Commander and organizational consultations, not to mention the ongoing responsibilities involved in managing an outpatient practice.

There are some vicissitudes of military life that one needs to make peace with early on. From mandatory HIV testing to periodic random urinalysis, to dress code, hair length, and so on, military members agree to basic compromises with respect to the exercise of their civil rights. And, of course, when they tell you to move, you move, and there's not much room for negotiation.

Family members' alliance on these issues is absolutely critical. Support services are substantial, but unless one's spouse's career and lifestyle preferences are compatible with one's own and unless one's spouse can adapt to new environments—including at least one overseas living experience—the unpredictability and perforce relinquishment of control involved in military life can be quite stressful.

Military service is now voluntary, and I still very much miss the infusion of our ranks with graduates of civilian residency training programs each summer. These days we train the vast majority of our new psychiatrists in our own residency programs, and these people, by and large, come to us after having participated in sponsored medical student programs. Thus, most of our new psychiatrists have had at least seven years in uniform by the time they are first eligible to leave the military.

The actuarial tables apparently indicate that, if you are in uniform for around ten years, the 20-year retirement income and ancillary benefits are such that completing a career makes sound financial sense. Most of our members will be so eligible at about age 45, still midcareer for a psychiatrist. If you are a "Regular" officer, you get to stay for 30 years!

The career tracks available are varied so I will discuss only the most popular. Those interested in academic psychiatry will, out of residency training, begin the board certification process at an assignment usually at a smaller facility. If the person is interested in fellowship training, she or he may well volunteer at this time for an overseas tour so as to complete this requirement early on. Once board certification is attained, along with an initial operational tour, fellowship application generally occurs next. There are two venues: first, military sponsorship, wherein one's military salary continues at the staff rate; second, one requests "redeferred" status, wherein one is released from active service for the duration of the training. The first option carries a service-time obligation; the second does not. Child, forensic, psychopharmacology, and research psychiatry fellowship programs have been the most frequently subscribed.

After certification in adult psychiatry, and then fellowship training, assignment to a facility with a psychiatry residency training program generally follows. These are not "publish or perish" environments, but rather ones wherein teaching and clinical work are emphasized. Assignment to the Uniformed Services School of Medicine is possible for those with an academic interest in research on the stress disorders.

Career progression from smaller facilities with only outpatient services to regional hospitals and on to medical centers, with greater degrees of administrative responsibility, is the most usual career track. Most people make up their minds where they want to settle and arrange a terminal assignment near that location.

There are surprises at every turn. It is a frequent occurrence to hear that someone was assigned to a location under some duress, only to hear later that the person wishes to settle in that location. The categories of one's experience are limited, and so the obligatory adaptation that military life evokes can open new vistas. Trust me that this is true!

Money is an issue. With the enfranchisement of the "all volunteer force," Congress realized that there would have to be some economic incentive to a career in military medicine. The template used was the salaries in academic medicine, since they corresponded roughly to the rank structure within the military. The base salary is determined by one's rank (grade "0–3," Captain in the Army and Air Force, and Lieutenant in the Navy are the entry ranks for physicians). There is a $500 monthly additive just for being a physician, a $4000–$5000 per year additive for being board certified, $1500 per year "Additional Special Pay" for signing for one year, and additional specialty bonuses for signing for longer periods of time. There are also "Cost of Living" increases in high-cost areas like the nation's Capital, and quarters and subsistence allowances, which are paid monthly. These allowances are tax-free income, and if a member claims a state of residence that does not tax military pay, then the member pays only Federal income tax. The salary structure is thus very competitive with that which psychiatrists earn in the private sector and are without the burdens of office expense and malpractice insurance overhead. Retirement pay is calculated as a fraction of "base pay," that is, without bonuses or allowances for a given rank. Following 20 years of service, the rate is approximately 50%, and after 30 years it is approximately 75%, of base pay.

There are also ways to take only half a loaf. There are two kinds of reservists. One kind is assigned to a unit, which, when deployed for training or duty, takes the psychiatrist, who is, in the Air Force, generally trained additionally as a flight surgeon. The other kind is called an "Individual Mobilization Augmentee." This person is assigned to a specific position (e.g., the Chairperson of Psychiatry at a medical center) and makes her or his arrangements for time spent on active duty with the incumbent of that position. These billets are generally filled by people who have a special expertise or by those who have had prior service. Finally, there are the elements of the National Guard, which are under state control.

Military psychiatrists have substantial corporate responsibilities which include evaluating members who are referred for clearance to work with nuclear or conventional weapons, to have security clearances of various levels, to be allowed to work around highly placed government officials, to operate high-performance aircraft, and so on. Forensic, competency, and disability determinations are another part of one's routine caseload. We teach our psychiatrists how to synthesize their responsibilities to both their patients and to the Air Force and make clear that what is truly best for the patient will, in the end, be best for the Service.

Being a part of the military changes, over time, your notions about being an American. To witness the assembly of an Air Transportable Hospital from vacant lot to open-for-business halfway around the world on next to no notice, engenders some understanding of how America is seen by other nations. Seven four-story-high aircraft appear on the horizon, and the next thing you see is that everything, from operating rooms to mental health modules, is in use. Transport jets with Red Crosses begin to load and unload patients as if the hospital had been operating for years. Host-country observers, military or not, stand back in awe. For most of them, this is all of America they will ever see in person—how we take care of our own and others in time of need.

As managed care has changed the landscape of practice opportunities for psychiatrists nationally, we have experienced an increased interest in military psychiatry. It is important to understand that utilization management tools are in active use within the services. The Department of Defense uses Health Management Strategies International, Inc. utilization review criteria for all its mental health services within its facilities, as it mandates their use by CHAMPUS providers in the private sector. Some mission-related clinical problems may obtain exemption from their application, but such exemptions occur only on an individual-case basis.

The future will bring an increasing number of facilities, especially within metropolitan areas, that are staffed by members of all three military services. This is already the case overseas. A "purple" uniform[1] is unlikely in the near term because of the special clinical support needs each service will continue to generate, but an experience of joint service will almost certainly be a part of the career of all those currently serving.

For certain kinds of people, military service can indeed allow them to "aim high" and to "be more than they can be," while doing what is much "more than a job."

RECOMMENDED READING

Jones, F. D., ed. (1994), *Textbook of Military Psychiatry, Part I: Warfare, Weaponry, and the Casualty*. Washington, DC: Office of the

---

[1]A universal, triservice uniform instead of Air Force Blue, Army Green, etc.

Surgeon General, Borden Institute, Walter Reed Army Medical Center.

Menninger, W. W. (1987), Military psychiatry: Learning from experience. *Bull. Menninger Clin.*, 51:3–5.

Military Psychiatry: A Tri-Service Perspective. Proceedings of the Operational Problems in the Behavioral Sciences Symposium (1984). Brooks Air Force Base.

Ursano, R. J., Holloway, H. C., Jones, D.R., et al. (1989), Psychiatric care in the military community: Family and military stressors. *Hosp. Community Psychiat.*, 40:1284–1289.

11

Legal Regulation of Practice

[FORENSIC PSYCHIATRY]

Robert L. Sadoff

Dr. Sadoff is Clinical Professor of Psychiatry at the University of Pennsylvania School of Medicine, Philadelphia. He also directs the Forensic Psychiatric Clinic and the Center for Studies in Social-Legal Psychiatry at the University of Pennsylvania. Having left his treatment practice after about 20 years, he was one of the first psychiatrists in the United States to practice full-time forensic psychiatry. Dr. Sadoff has been a pioneer in the changing field of forensic psychiatry and was one of the original founders, and served as the second president, of the American Academy of Psychiatry and the Law. He also helped found the American Board of Forensic Psychiatry and served as its fifth president. He has also served on the founding board of the Added Qualifications in Forensic Psychiatry of the American Board of Psychiatry and Neurology. Dr. Sadoff has written several books and over 100 papers and chapters on forensic psychiatry. He has lectured in virtually every state in the United States and in 12 other countries of the world. He is internationally known for his work in forensic psychiatry and has had various cases referred to him from different countries. He is the recipient of the Earl Bond Award for Outstanding Teaching in the Department of Psychiatry at the University of Pennsylvania; the Nathaniel Winkelman Award for outstanding contributions to the field of psychiatry; and the Manfred Guttmacher Award for his book entitled, *Psychiatric Malpractice: Cases and Comments for Clinicians* (co-authored with Robert Simon). He is also the recent recipient of the Phillipe Pinel Award of the International Academy of Law and Mental Health.

The practice of psychiatry has changed drastically over the past four decades. People have referred to the third revolution in psychiatry, which has been marked by legal regulation, a significant rise in psychiatric malpractice cases, and an appreciation for the rights of psychiatric patients. All these changes have come rather rapidly and have been confusing to a number of practicing psychiatrists. Formerly psychiatrists were truly in charge of their patients; they made decisions for their patients. Currently, third-party payers, regulatory agencies, lawyers, and judges intrude on the practice of psychiatry. A number of psychiatrists have turned to the study of law to help understand these changes in regulation and implementation that profoundly affected the practice of psychiatry.

HISTORICAL ANTECEDENTS

Early forensic psychiatrists were often referred to as alienists and limited their practice to criminal cases where insanity was pled or to civil cases where competency was an issue. With the rise of regulatory changes, beginning in the 1960s, however, the role of forensic psychiatrists has expanded. To comply with standards of care and avoid malpractice claims, forensic psychiatrists have been called on by colleagues to translate and understand the new regulations that were imposed on psychiatric treatment.

The concepts of right to treatment, right to refuse treatment, patients' rights and autonomy, and informed consent all served to confuse practicing psychiatrists who needed to make abrupt changes in the way they practiced psychiatry. The Tarasoff case in California in the mid-1970s also imposed a challenge to practicing psychiatrists when the patient threatened to harm an identified third party. In that case, the psychiatrist was obliged to warn or protect the third party threatened by the patient. Breaching of confidentiality was opposed by most psychiatrists, who could not understand this mandate by the Supreme Court of California and subsequently by other courts throughout the country.

Most recently, lawsuits against psychiatrists treating young women who harbor repressed memories of sexual abuse and then sue their fathers and others whom they believe harmed them when they were younger has also confused psychiatrists, who believed their patients were truthful and required continued treatment.

Thus, the field of forensic psychiatry has proliferated significantly over the past 30 to 40 years. We have seen the rise of the American Academy of Psychiatry and the Law, which started with eight members in 1969 and currently has over 1,500 active members. The American Board of Forensic Psychiatry has certified almost 300 forensic psychiatrists in its 20 years of operation. Even with the current added qualifications, forensic psychiatry is receiving a large number of applicants for its examinations. The numbers of individuals involved in court proceedings has risen, as have the number of journals relating specifically to law and psychiatry. The field has grown beyond its original boundaries involving insanity and competency, to include a number of criminal issues, especially cases of murder, sexual crimes, drug- and alcohol-related crimes, and other criminal behavior where mental illness becomes an issue. Forensic psychiatrists in criminal cases have been asked to evaluate individuals not only for competency to stand trial, but for competency to give a confession or to waive their Miranda rights and to plead, to be sentenced, or to be executed.

Perhaps the greatest growth for forensic psychiatrists has occurred in civil cases, wherein the traditional issues of testamentary capacity have been supplemented with other areas of competency, including testimonial capacity, competency to enter into contracts, competency to raise children, and other domestic relations issues. Also coming under the purview of forensic psychiatrists are industrial matters, including sexual harassment at work, and gender, racial, and political discrimination, which may lead to emotional disturbance. Physical injuries that have resulted in emotional damage are often referred for psychiatric evaluation. Class actions involving toxic tort, nuclear spills, and other major disasters that affect mental health have been assessed by forensic psychiatrists. Automobile accidents and plane crashes affecting individuals and families have been referred to forensic psychiatrists for evaluation and treatment. Medical and psychiatric malpractice cases have also become a part of the forensic psychiatrist's area of expertise.

The field is growing, it is open, and it is one in which a psychiatrist may still earn a decent living without excessive regulation or imposed managed care, as is the case for the treating psychiatrists. There are, however, a number of psychiatrists who have always been frightened by lawyers and courts and wish to avoid forensic psychiatric cases like

the plague. They eschew the problems of regulation and fear domina-
tion by the courts and others in cross-examination of their work.
Psychiatrists have historically been free of external questioning of
their treatment methods and modalities. In forensic work, a psychiatrist may be under scrutiny to explain, under lengthy and intense
cross-examination, his or her treatment or assessment or diagnosis.

MY INVOLVEMENT IN FORENSIC PSYCHIATRY

I started out thinking about who actually sees people who have
emotional problems before they get to psychiatrists. I considered three
major groups: taxi drivers, bartenders, and attorneys. I believed it
would be more difficult to work with the first two groups, so I thought
the problems that were brought to attorneys by people with legal
problems might also have psychiatric implications. I spoke to a
number of lawyers during my residency, and they confirmed my
suspicions. They found that they, indeed, had to be counselors as well
as attorneys and looked for psychiatrists who would be willing to work
with them. They found much resistance among our colleagues, who
considered lawyers as threatening and controlling. I attended commitment hearings in the courts in Los Angeles and found them to be
superficial and without comprehensive assessment. I also found that
the courts were willing to go along with the "30-second" examinations
by the two psychiatrists appointed by the court to evaluate individuals
for their need for hospitalization.

I thought about taking a fellowship in forensic psychiatry, one of
the few that existed in the early 1960s. But I was on the Berry plan,
under which the Army allowed me to complete my residency before
I had to begin service in the United States Army. While at Ft. Dix,
New Jersey, I volunteered to do all the courts martial and stockade
psychiatry that existed on the base. I also took an afternoon off to
study with Dr. Melvin Heller and Professor Sam Polsky at the Unit in
Law and Psychiatry at Temple University. It was that experience that
stimulated my interest and development in forensic psychiatry. I was
named as the first Clinical Director of the State Maximum Security
Forensic Diagnostic Hospital at Holmesburg Prison and also served as
consultant in forensic psychiatry to the Norristown State Hospital for

10 years. Those experiences enhanced my interest in forensic and correctional psychiatry. Perhaps the greatest impetus, though, came from my colleagues, who were delighted that the "masochist" was in town to take the legal cases off their hands. Most psychiatrists in the early 1960s did not wish to become involved in legal matters (perhaps the same is still true). They referred all lawyers to me because I was willing to take these cases.

As my forensic practice grew and my writings contributed to my academic and intellectual growth in the field, I changed from Temple University Medical and Law School positions to a position at the University of Pennsylvania, when Jonas Robitscher left for Atlanta, Georgia. I developed the Center for Studies in Social-Legal Psychiatry with my administrative assistant, Dorothy Gottlieb, who came out of the business world, where she had supervised the work of more than 200 people for several years. She proved to be an excellent coordinator and administrator, and we did research through NIMH grants, teaching in various parts of the medical school, including Child Psychiatry, Marriage Council, Philadelphia General Hospital, and the Residency Program for several years. At the same time, I also taught a course in psychiatry and law at the Villanova University School of Law.

My work at the University of Pennsylvania at the present time is limited to one day a week, when I volunteer my time to teach the residents and other residents from various programs in and around Philadelphia. We see patients in our Forensic Psychiatry Clinic, and the residents learn how to write a good forensic psychiatric report. We also take field trips to various forensic and correctional institutions in the area and speak with judges, prosecutors, and defense attorneys to obtain their perspective on cases in which they are involved. I also share with the residents my clinical experience and invite them to come to court whenever they are able.

There are about 20 accredited forensic psychiatric fellowship programs throughout the country where residents spend one full year in training with a board certified forensic psychiatrist and other professional staff. A number of my residents have gone on to take formal fellowship training in forensic psychiatry, and many of them have distinguished themselves in the field. In 1994, during the American Psychiatric Association meetings in Philadelphia, I hosted a reunion of all of the people that I had trained over the past 25 years and was delighted with the number of practicing forensic psychiatrists and the degree of experience and expertise they have developed.

LAW SCHOOL

Many persons ask whether or not a forensic psychiatrist needs to go to law school to practice this subspecialty in psychiatry. I have encouraged young people to attend law school whenever they can because it is important for them to have a perspective on the field of law, to understand how lawyers approach problems and how they think about various cases. I did attend law school, but I had the privilege of going without the need to obtain a degree back in the early 60s. I have not wished to obtain a law degree myself and do not feel that I need it. A number of my colleagues are dually degreed and find that this is an advantage in their work; but it can also be a disadvantage if the psychiatrist/attorney is asked legal questions when testifying as a mental health expert.

FORENSIC PSYCHOLOGY

It is important to note the existence of the forensic psychologists as well, since their numbers have grown over the past several decades. There are national organizations and board certifications for forensic psychologists. Forensic psychiatrists should be aware of the good psychologists in the area who are willing to do this kind of work. It is often important to work closely with a forensic psychologist when developing a particular criminal or civil case.

CONCLUSION

The field of psychiatry has changed drastically over the past several years, requiring the knowledge of law and legal regulations of our practice. Recently, with the advent of managed care, a number of psychiatrists are feeling the pinch in their private practice and are turning to other areas of professional work to supplement their income. A number have turned to forensic psychiatry, and I have seen a proliferation of applications for my course and for the fellowships in forensic psychiatry throughout the country. It is important for those psychiatrists who testify in court to have some knowledge of forensic principles so that they conduct themselves properly in court. A number of books are informative, and there is a course that is given by the American Academy of Psychiatry and the Law for sharpening one's skills in this particular area.

I strongly urge any psychiatrist who has an interest in the law or in the various aspects of psychiatry that touch on the law to consider forensic psychiatry as a subspecialty or to supplement his or her psychiatric work with forensic cases. Forensic psychiatry has also grown through the mentorship program. A number of forensic psychiatrists that I know will work directly with young psychiatrists who wish to learn more about this fascinating field. I often get calls from colleagues asking questions about Tarasoff issues, treatment issues, competency issues, confidentiality matters, and the like. I'm happy to consult with them informally by telephone and also formally in person.

RECOMMENDED READING

Bursten, B. (1984), *Beyond Psychiatric Expertise.* Springfield, IL: Thomas.

Committee on Psychiatry and the Law for the Group for the Advancement of Psychiatry (1991), *The Mental Health Professional and the Legal System, Report #131.* New York: Brunner/Mazel.

Halleck, S. L. (1980), *Law in the Practice of Psychiatry: A Handbook for Clinicians.* New York: Plenum Press.

Rosner, R., ed. (1994), *Principles and Practice of Forensic Psychiatry.* New York: Chapman & Hall.

Sadoff, R. L. (1988), *Forensic Psychiatry: A Practical Guide for Lawyers and Psychiatrists,* 2nd ed. Springfield, IL: Thomas.

Simon, R. I. (1992), *Clinical Psychiatry and the Law,* 2nd Edition. Washington, DC: American Psychiatric Press.

Simon, R. I., & Sadoff, R. L. (1992), *Psychiatric Malpractice: Cases and Comments for Clinicians.* Washington, DC: American Psychiatric Press.

✳ 12 ✳

Transition to a New Kind of Academia: Pharmaceutical Medicine, Pharmaceutical R&D

[THE PHARMACEUTICAL INDUSTRY]

Gary D. Tollefson

Dr. Tollefson is a Vice President of Lilly Research Laboratories, a division of Eli Lilly and Company. He leads a fully dedicated, cross-functional global development team responsible for the corporation's innovative new anti-psychotic medication, olanzapine. His current position is the result of an early midcareer move. Prior to this move, Dr. Tollefson was Chairman of the Department of Psychiatry at the St. Paul Ramsey Medical Center/ Ramsey Clinic in St. Paul, Minnesota, and an Associate Professor in Psychiatry at the University of Minnesota Medical School, Minneapolis. During that time he was involved in several diverse pursuits, including research, teaching, administration, patient care, and innovative mental health and substance abuse program development. Dr. Tollefson graduated summa cum laude in psychology and obtained his M.D. and Ph.D. degrees from the University of Minnesota Medical School. He has written over 100 articles and numerous book chapters and monographs and is a frequent spokesperson at national and international scientific symposia.

It was a dark and stormy evening. As the psychiatrist entered his office, unaware of the magnitude of the threat awaiting only a few feet away, he paused. The room was still. A strange odor permeated the senses, musty, aged, and strangely reminiscent. After a few moments, still captured in a subliminal sense of foreboding, the doctor turned on the lights. Ahhhh!!!! A shriek pierced the evening like a saber slashing the finest of silk. There, before the tired and drawn healer, stood the

129

Beast. The Beast was inanimate. It was endless stacks of charts, piles of phone messages, prescription renewal requests, unopened correspondence, grant proposals, manuscripts in preparation, hospital policy and procedure manuals, budget sheets . . . you get the point. Life in academic medicine was fun. Past tense may be a bit unfair; I suppose it still can be. And experience as an academic researcher, teacher, clinician, and administrator builds a tremendous career foundation. But after a while, the phrase "been there, done it" rings all too real. In our current health care environment, change is the only constant. The practice of academic medicine was becoming less fun, not like "the good old days." In my case, dissonance eventually led to change. The transition to a major new challenge, in an enriched environment dedicated to achieving tangible research and better health care solutions for patients, was seductive. But first, the background.

EARLY EXPERIENCES

When I completed my psychiatric residency, I began working at a major teaching hospital as an instructor. I was fortunate to have completed my Ph.D. thesis (in psychopharmacology) while working on the consultation-liaison (C-L) service. Both of these early professional experiences merit comment. If the opportunity to obtain a second degree is available, consider it! A scientific or clinical Ph.D., while certainly not mandatory, is valuable. An appreciation and knowledge of "the bench" benefits one on either an academic or an industrial pharmaceutical track. From facilitating grantspersonship to being a foundation for cross-functional communication, the Ph.D. is undeniably an asset. If a doctorate doesn't seem right, consider an M.B.A. Our profession is increasingly a business. An understanding of the marketplace and the forces shaping it, and having the confidence to participate in reform, bring a skillset useful in any type of practice.

I found C-L psychiatry to be a superb experience. The challenge to remain contemporary in other medical disciplines, to learn to communicate effectively across functions, and to understand the interface of psyche and soma is unparalleled. While the experience may not be for everyone, those who partake in it develop transferrable skills such as decision analysis, the ability to communicate your discipline to others who haven't your background, to listen, and to deliver a series of recommendations tailored to your individual customer. So why leave it?

NAVIGATING WITH A BROKEN COMPASS

I found that, as my career progressed, the opportunities (a.k.a. the demands) grew exponentially while my available time shrank. Superimposed were the simultaneous changes occurring in the world of health care. These stressors were further multiplied when I became a department chairperson. Reality felt as if there were more than four directions on the compass and I was headed in each one at the same time!

Lesson number one: whatever you do, don't forget to set limits. While it may not be in our nature – and it is certainly not emphasized as part of our training – you must learn to say NO!! Quality of life can be, perhaps all too often is, an endangered species in medicine. Seek a balance, don't forget to have fun, and don't neglect those you need the most! End of sermon.

My academic career was putting me on the path to "burnout." In retrospect, I'm not sure how many of those contributing factors would have been controllable. The ultimate sum of more and more clinic demands to support salary, prospecting for the next grant, struggling to find adequate time to write, attempting to understand, accommodate to, and proactively change hospital bureaucracy, recruit, develop staff, deal with facilities issues, teach, travel to present data, . . . oh well, you get the idea. The bottom line was that expectations kept climbing, time was waning, and the enjoyment – the fire – wasn't burning as brightly.

I had been a consultant to the pharmaceutical industry for some time before I ever considered it as a career option. Conducting clinical trials with new compounds in development or new applications for those already in the marketplace, consulting on medical challenges facing a corporation, and writing educational material can be ways to both get exposure to the industry as a whole and begin to assess differentially the philosophies, values, research programs, and the people from one company to the next. These attributes vary, and I certainly found significant between-company differences ($p < .0001$).

Companies are heterogenous. The drug industry is no exception. What is the set of shared values held by the company? What is its history and current commitment to research and development in your discipline? Within the decision-making process, what degree of influence and participation does the science group possess? What is the degree of commitment to your career development by the human resource organization? These are but a few of the questions you should ask. But, on the bright side, how many HMOs, university departments, clinics, have the time, resources, and commitment to help you personally develop and prosper?

But a career with one of the drug companies? Come on . . . Nobody with any qualifications works there. Yeah, it was okay to get a few books, some pizza, maybe even a stethoscope, but a career?? The risk of corruption, immorality, materialism, and inhumanity—you've got to be kidding!

As psychiatrists, we deplore stereotypes. In fact, we work every day to destigmatize our patients, their diseases, and our own profession. So why react negatively to a pharmaceutical-based research career? Our colleagues in the basic sciences, such as chemistry, biology, and statistics, view these finite career opportunities as "jewels." Perhaps a combination of selective exposure to but one aspect of a company (sales) and ignorance about pharmaceutical research and development (R&D) has kept this an unknown secret.

A JOB OPENING

Consider the following job announcement: "Opening within a research-based organization devoting one billion dollars annually to its research programs. World-class facilities and state-of-the-art technical support. Opportunity to work with novel pharmacologic probes and innovative protocol development with improved health care outcomes as your objective. With medical research in over 30 countries this is a unique chance to be part of a diverse global research team. A substantive commitment to your individual career growth. Competitive salary, excellent fringe benefits, reasonable hours, and the chance to develop an equity position (part ownership) in the organization." Not bad! This and more is why a career in pharmaceutical medicine merits your consideration.

Unfortunately nobody laid it out quite like that for me. After I consulted for a major U.S. pharmaceutical company on a then growing controversy, the conversation for career possibilities began. I had just had the chance to review a tremendous clinical data base and saw a plethora of research hypotheses before my eyes. One of those turned out to be the key to my host's quandary. Cloistered with a diverse group of bright, talented, and energetic scientists, physicians, attorneys, statisticians, and market executives, I actually had some time to think! We sat around and brainstormed. We had the necessary statistical support to get quick answers. We could actually get something done relatively expeditiously. Eureka! Bureaucracy wasn't everywhere; some people were actually goal oriented and empowered or had the resources to make it happen. A novel paradigm—the way it should be! But not reality in most practice or academic settings. Hmmm? Maybe the source of my recent frustrations was the gap between what I wanted to get done and what I actually could get done!! Not rocket science, rather what we psychiatrists call insight! While it might not be a cure, I could at least see symptom attenuation in that kind of work environment.

Over the next four months I was aggressively recruited. I made three separate visits to better understand this company and how I might fit in. Still, there was lingering doubt. Maybe a bird in the hand was worth two in the bush. Yeah, the grass is greener . . . I dictated my letter to decline their offer. The biggest obstacle was probably fear of change. That's when fate (or at least AT&T) intervened. That morning, before the mail left my office, the phone rang. It was the president of Lilly Research Laboratories, who actually wanted to know what more they could do! His suggestions were compelling, and, before I knew it, the first day of the rest of my life began.

In retrospect, I think obstacles to change were there merely to give me adequate time to pause and reflect. In order to change you need first to know yourself. Informed consent means gathering all the relevant facts and then critically assessing the benefits versus the risks of change. If the gap is too narrow and the decisions too hard, determine what you need to shift the ratio. Then go out and ask for it!

Be assertive if you're worth it, but don't lose sight of reality. There may also be something to timing. If the worst-case scenario follows your decision to change, it is nice to be young enough to return or mature in career to have the freedom to continue to explore. Ideally, a move to a pharmaceutical R&D career might be best after a few years of academic experience (entry position) or after establishing a senior track record of research and administration (advanced position). Having worked with patients and their families in "the real world" and having conducted clinical trials provide unique skills that few can bring to the pharmaceutical industry. Representing the patient's need is what we know best as clinicians.

THE JOB DESCRIPTION

What does a Clinical Research Physician do in the industry? Many opportunities exist. A short list includes basic science ("the bench"), pharmacology, clinical trials, health economics, disease management, information technology, market development, and regulatory (e.g., FDA relations). A person's career path may involve one or a combination of several of these options. Most large companies will permit some movement across areas over time, which is nice diversity for those who like changes and new challenges periodically. Some of the strategic dimensions representing the expectations in a pharmaceutical medicine position include:

- *Technical competency.* You must possess, and continue to develop, the functional and technical skills in your discipline necessary to design, monitor, and analyze clinical research.
- *Effective communication.* Communication skills are perhaps among the most important attributes to succeed in this role. Regardless of the medium, the ability to present complicated information from your discipline in a simple, straightforward, and persuasive style is critical. The reciprocal skill set is the gift of actively listening to others, understanding their issues, and incorporating their perspectives to achieve consensus eventually. While certainly much communication occurs one-on-one, the reality in the industry is that key decisions

generate from group interactions. If you think reasonably well on your feet and share the wisdom of your ideas effectively, you've taken a BIG STEP!

- *Relationship building.* The stimulus of this type of position derives from the diversity (training, professional, global, ethnic, etc.) of your colleagues. As you convey their medical expertise, be ready to learn much yourself. I didn't appreciate the real complexity of pharmacological research (not to mention drug development and market support) until being exposed to so many professionals of varying backgrounds. Each contributes an essential component to ensure that the final outcome maximizes benefits to the patient. To participate successfully as a team contributor, one must build and maintain strong, lasting relationships based on a mutual platform of shared values. Effectively leveraging your team's diversity undoubtedly improves effectiveness. So the question is, what do you do to create an environment where people want to and are able to get involved?

- *Personal commitment.* The ability to demonstrate a strong personal drive to achieve results, be resilient, and make calculated decisions with an overriding commitment to the integrity and quality of work you do is important. While certainly not unique to this position, it is critical to know the limits of your abilities and seek input when necessary. A helpful hint is to be flexible, open to change, and able to cope with ambiguity because it is all around us every day!!

- *Leadership.* It's relatively easy to *manage* people and processes, but the real challenge is to *lead* within an organization. What's the difference? A leader inspires those around him or her, models a set of values to others, engages and mobilizes commitment to an idea, is not afraid to challenge the status quo, and takes a clear stand in the face of conflict. This may sound like a very special breed of person. But if you strive to hold your interactions and behaviors up to such a standard, you may be surprised. And if you are successful, rewards aren't far behind.

- *Innovation and creativity.* This skill set should be self-evident. Innovation and continuous improvement can place you at the cutting edge of your field. In general, take what already exists and apply it effectively to new problems and situations by making key connections, or "bridging" ideas, from two or more different areas.

That's one recipe for success. It represents my own personal score card for what I do (or try to) each day in my position. As with any muscle group, regular exercise will help these basics to develop and become a style characterizing your work. While these are utilitarian outside of a pharmaceutical career, within industry, the opportunity to implement them, and the recognition that can follow, is second to none.

CONCLUSION

My story is almost over except for a couple of concluding remarks. Has this midcareer move changed my life? Absolutely! Am I content? No, but then I'm not sure I will ever be (or for that matter really want to be)! But I am definitely happier. You really can't beat playing in the major leagues, and once on the playing field you'll likely never leave. You've already chosen what you want to do. Now the real question is, where to do it? Give serious thought to an environment committed to innovative research to better the lives of millions and to providing the resources (human, technical, and financial) to make it happen. Would I do it differently? Not really. Maybe a little less kicking and scream-ing that first year (second guessing can be hazardous to your health). Maybe spending more energy working within a system and less searching for a perfect world. Probably appreciating sooner what leadership is and then doing it! Recognizing my limitations, appreci-ating my accomplishments. Finding that balance between one's pro-fessional and personal needs. These are a few of my learning points. Don't be afraid to explore and learn more about your most important research subject—yourself! Good luck.

RECOMMENDED READING

Rudnick, S. A., & Rosenthal, A. S. (1993), Research-organization and management philosophies: Their impact on physicians in academia and industry. In: *Future Practice Alternatives in Medicine,* 2nd ed., ed. D. Nash. New York: Igaku-Shoin, pp. 191–202.

Spilker, B. (1989), Career opportunities for physicians in the pharmaceutical industry. *J. Clin. Pharmacol.,* 29:1069–1076.

Power, Politics and the Psychiatrist

[ORGANIZED MEDICINE]

Paul Jay Fink

Dr. Fink is Senior Consultant to Charter Fairmount Behavioral Health System and Mustard Seed, Inc. and a professor in the department of psychiatry at Temple University School of Medicine. He is a past president of the American Psychiatric Association (APA), and serves as a member of its Board of Trustees. The APA has honored Dr. Fink by awarding him the Vestermark Award for teaching excellence and the Francis J. Braceland Award for public service. In addition, he has received numerous national and local honors for his work in organized medicine and psychiatry. Dr. Fink has published over 140 articles and has delivered more than 700 lectures across the United States, as well as internationally, on topics ranging from psychiatric education to economic problems facing modern psychiatry, the relationship between psychiatry and primary care, stigma against the mentally ill and their caretakers, violence and psychoanalysis. Dr. Fink is widely regarded as a national spokesperson for psychiatry and has been an invited guest on national and local television shows and radio programs.

Over the years I have thought a great deal about how careers in medicine are developed. Because of the path that my own career took, I have been curious to learn how people determine where they are going, what their interests are, and how they are going to pursue their own personal goals. Although there are notable exceptions to the following generalization, I believe that it is almost impossible to predict in advance what the course of your professional life will be and where you might end up.

In my own case, I started out believing that I would be in analytic practice full time and aspired during my residency to be a training analyst. A mixture of a person's own habits and beliefs, traits, and characteristics along with external events, both accidental and contrived, comprises the ingredients for career development. As a medical student and resident I was extremely naive. I had no idea what the difference between a good residency and a bad residency would mean, and I also had no thought of leaving Philadelphia. Some friends, I later learned, were interested in prestigious schools like Harvard and Yale for residency training or in research at NIMH. None of those things was either enticing or part of my plans. Frankly, I didn't even know about them. My search for a residency program was limited and was partially determined by my being married and poor and looking for a place where I could start to make a living. A cousin of my wife's suggested that I should not take the residency that paid the most at a state hospital, and he arranged for me to have a residency at a private hospital well regarded in this city. That was the first of a number of turning points ultimately affecting my career.

Characteristics that would influence my career included a penchant for hard work, an ability to teach, and the quality of being a maverick—outspoken and wishing to make things better. I also have lived by a personal philosophy that has had enormous influence on decisions that I've made concerning myself and my career: I don't like to be on the outside of the bakery with my nose pressed to the window; I like to be inside and included. That trait among many has been an important driving force in my organizational work throughout the years and has resulted in very positive feelings and activities, but also a lot of painful realities.

THE ROLE OF THE MENTOR

None of the important steps in my career would have occurred if I had not had an interested and influential mentor early in my career. After two years of practice as a full-time psychotherapist, I felt lonely, isolated, and in need of some external stimulation. I sought a faculty appointment at Hahnemann Medical College, since my assessment was that it had the best department of psychiatry in Philadelphia at the time. The chairman, Van Buren Osler Hammett, became my guide, mentor, and helper in the first decade of my career. I volunteered two hours a week and was given an assignment to teach medical students at Philadelphia General Hospital (the city hospital at that time). A year and a half later I was a full-time member of the faculty and grew from the head of continuing education with some teaching responsibility to the head of all education of the department. Within eight years I went from instructor to professor. Notwithstanding my own energy and talents, it could never have happened without the kind and determined guidance of Dr. Hammett. He quietly but carefully shaped my career not only for my own good, but in his opinion for the good of the department. I was eager to please and willing to work hard, and he was willing to give me freedom to grow and the opportunity to use my creativity in a number of places that would not have been possible without his guidance and his willingness to share the spotlight. I learned to be a mentor from him. He was frank, thoughtful, and a great politician and he furthered my career.

Several experiences during the 60s were, in retrospect, very influential. In 1965 there were 13 or 14 departments of psychiatry that were highly dependent on, and very involved with, the development of the community mental health centers. Dr. Hammett was part of a small group of chairmen of such departments in an organization called FOG (Future-Oriented Group), and when the meeting took place in Philadelphia he invited me to be an observer. I think it would be more realistic to say a "go-fer." I never viewed it negatively, though. Sitting with people who had achieved high places in organized psychiatry, I was thrilled by the discussion, the ideas, and the enthusiasm of men embarking on a very interesting mission, that is, to bring community mental health and academic psychiatry together. That may have been the first national meeting I attended, and it was in no way a seminal meeting other than serving as a stimulus for my own interest in doing things on a larger scale.

Shortly after the FOG meeting I became involved in a local political activity called Lower Merion Citizens for Better Schools (CBS). The Superintendent of Schools for Lower Merion, an affluent suburb of Philadelphia, was retiring and there was a small group of us who wanted to ensure that we had at the helm a better person than had been there for the previous 30 years. Through a tremendous amount of letter writing and attempting to influence the situation politically, and with the help of a school board member who was very interested in our agenda, we were able to create a level of noise that allowed for a significant change. My political activity in CBS ultimately led to my being invited to be a member of the school board of Lower Merion Township, my first civic pro bono activity and one that would influence me immensely to take on similar activities in later years.

In 1969 Dr. Hammett indicated that the American College of Psychiatrists, a relatively new organization, was interested in getting younger people into the organization and invited me to become a member. That was another major turning point in my career. It allowed me a level of exposure and an opportunity to be with the national leaders which I craved, although I was not totally conscious of the craving. Because I was immersed in academic activity, organizing programs for medical students, graduate education for residents, and continuing education for people in the field, I began to participate actively in national organizations and was rewarded by having an opportunity to become part of the APA, and to participate in the development of the AAP (Association of Academic Psychiatry) and other key groups.

INVOLVEMENT IN ORGANIZED PSYCHIATRY

My entry into the American Psychiatric Association was a combination of naivete and brashness. I thought I ought to be on the Council of Medical Education and Career Development. I had no idea how the APA operated and went straight ahead to seek an appointment. I found out who was the Chair of the Council at that time— Bernie Holland, Chairman of Psychiatry at Emory University—called him up, and suggested that I ought to be appointed. In retrospect, I can say that he had enormous patience and a willingness to be a guide. He asked me if I was going to the next annual meeting of the APA and suggested that we meet and talk. At that meeting he carefully told me that he had no control over appointments, that the president-elect did the appointing, and that he thought it was interesting that I wanted to be on the Council and talked to me about it. Through his efforts I was later appointed to a committee for medical students, ultimately was appointed to the Council on Medical Education and Career Development, and finally chaired that Council in the late 70s. I am not sure how I would have gotten into the APA structure without that boost from Dr. Holland, but I know that there are others who find sponsors in a less brash and more organized way.

Once I got involved, my willingness to be outspoken and make waves called notice to me. Then I was off on a very heady career in the APA, starting as a committee member and moving through a number of positions including Chairman of the Council on Medical Education and Career Development, Chairman of the Joint Commission on Public Affairs, Vice President, and ultimately President. During the decade that those things took place, my position within the organization became much more secure. I became better known for a number of reasons and was able to move on through these positions owing to a number of political maneuvers I had learned through experience. Seeking office, seeking allies and friends, taking positions, and speaking out were critical parts of the next stage of my career.

THE AMERICAN COLLEGE OF PSYCHIATRISTS

Being a young Fellow at the ACP, I was overwhelmed by its membership and the high esteem in which many of its members were held. The meetings were filled with complex emotions of ambition, envy, and pride. The ACP prides itself on having the best continuing education programs of all psychiatric organizations, and I eagerly attended those programs. I envied the speakers and wished that I could be invited to be a speaker. In 1982 I finally got the chance and was given the stage. My speech was titled "The Ethics of Physicians in a For Profit World." This opportunity changed my career and set me off into the political arena. It was a very heady experience and somewhat frightening to speak to the elite of psychiatry on a subject about which I was very passionate. I was also concerned that in my zeal I would overstate my case. I worked harder on that speech than on almost any other I have ever given, and I would say that it paid off. My speech was, in many ways, an exhortation to the leadership of American psychiatry to insist on the highest ethical standards for our profession to ensure our survival in what were the beginnings of enormous changes in the fiscal structure of psychiatry which we now understand much better. Somehow I had the insight to see what was coming and gave a talk that people later said led to the greatest applause they had ever heard. It was an extremely successful moment and filled me with the ambition to move into political office as no other event in my life had done.

THE WISH TO BE A CHAIRMAN

In 1972 I became more interested in the idea of being a chairman. I wanted to be a chairman among chairmen, and I wanted to participate at those levels of discourse. I began to seek a chairmanship and was rewarded by an invitation to become a chairman at Eastern Virginia Medical School. In those years I saw myself as an academic and wanted to follow that career path. I began the search. I recall Dr. Hammett's response, which was another turning point and lesson for me, when I told him I wanted to be a department chairman. He asked me why, and I said, "Because you're a department chairman." He laughed and then said, "You know, there's a down side. I have 200 transferences going on simultaneously at all times that I have to deal with." Only by being in that position can one appreciate the wisdom of his remark. But I was determined, young, brash, and very willing to move out of Philadelphia if that's what it took to move along in the career path of a chairman.

In the ten years from my graduation from residency to my first chair, the idea of being a training analyst had long faded and the idea of moving along academic lines became much more intense. Being a chairman opened up a number of opportunities, and I again moved rapidly toward fulfilling myself by becoming part of the inside leadership group among the chairmen. Once again, this occurred as an accident. At my first meeting, the president of the organization, Danny Freedman, asked for a volunteer to serve as the organization's representative to the Council of Academic Societies (CAS) of the Association of American Medical Colleges. I eagerly volunteered without really understanding that the representative to the CAS was a permanent member of the Executive Committee of the American Association of Chairmen of Departments of Psychiatry. Thus, as presidents came and went, I remained on the Council and became an insider. How things might have gone if I had not volunteered I don't know, but, having done so, I was immediately boosted from a novice chairman to one of the ten leaders in this group of 120 men and women who were the academic leaders of American psychiatry. As the representative of the CAS, I stayed on and, for the full 12 years of being an academic chairman, I was on the Executive Committee. That tenure gave me a number of significant opportunities that added to my ability to rise in the field and achieve a significant number of presidencies of various professional organizations.

Three other personal characteristics pushed my career: impatience, a creative talent for putting things together and making things grow, and charisma. Eastern Virginia Medical School was a brand new school at which I was the first Clinical Chairman and the first Chairman of the Curriculum Committee. Having had significant curriculum committee experience at Hahnemann, I was prepared to write the entire curriculum for a new three-year school. This was at a time when the general feeling in our country was that we needed more doctors, so three-year schools were in vogue. My influence on the school was extensive, and I was not only proud of my accomplishments but also very proud of the growth of the school in those first few years. But the lure of going home and the invitation by Jefferson Medical College to be Chairman of Psychiatry there, an older, established school, was a more prestigious position and brought me back to Philadelphia in 1976.

PROS AND CONS OF HAVING A BIG MOUTH

As a psychiatric and medical politician, I have been outspoken on many issues over the past two decades. During my first month at Jefferson I suffered a serious attack of "foot in mouth" disease which was to affect my career for the rest of my time at Jefferson and even afterwards. This anecdote is instructive because it reveals one of the personal flaws that interfered with the full measure of development of an academic and political career that would flourish. The incident has to do with timing and appropriateness. The nature of politics is that one has to do things in order to win and not in order to be seen or noticed. At my first meeting of the Dean's Council of Chairmen, two psychologists were about to be admitted to the staff of Obstetrics and Gynecology to do sexual therapy. I opposed it and made a generalization that people with certain training should be in the department of their training and then lent out to the other departments or paid for by the other

departments. I was unaware that the entire department of family medicine consisted of non-family physicians. If my suggestion had been
adopted, it would have destroyed the Department of Family Medicine.
Both the Chairman of Family Medicine and the Dean were infuriated,
and it was reprimanded at the very beginning of my career there.

In contrast, I have noted in many committees and councils that
people can be present and yet never say a word. That silence also is a
failure in the use of the power inherent in membership. The issue of
power is important for those who wish to have a career in organized
medicine or psychiatry. It is clearly the most important motivator,
along with responsibility and creativity. There is a feeling of fulfillment that comes from being able to change policy, whether in
government, an organization, or an institution. The power to affect
policy and change the lives of a significant number of people is part of
the attraction of political medicine, and it is also part of the problem
in that it leads to enormous competition among powerful people.
Robert Petersdorf, former President of the Association of American
Medical Colleges, once said, "The reason that medical school politics
are so vicious is that the spoils are so few." The greatest deterent to
power and success is fear: one's own fears of failure, of reprimand, of
losing one's job, and of others who wish to curb your power. The more
fear there is, the more anxiety a person has and the less likely one is to
be willing to stick his neck out or be visible at the front of the column.

Most power is delegated. Since there is always someone who is
responsible for a person—some higher power, whether it's the dean,
the president of the hospital, the board—the issues surrounding power
have to do with whether, once it has been delegated, a person uses it.
As I review my career, I can see that I used it. Sometimes I took power
that I didn't have—for which l was restrained at times—and sometimes
I abused it. But I think that, for the most part, I was able to take the
power and creatively turn it into growth. My special area of expertise
is to create programs that flourish (and also make money) and to be in
positions that allow me to affect public or institutional policy.

RECOGNITION

Clearly, the path to success and fulfillment in the political arena is
recognition. Whether the recognition comes in the form of intrainsti-

tutional praise for developing a strong department that through the
vagaries of political competition within an organization lead to a rise
to the presidency or some other high office commanding recognition
by one's colleagues, or whether it is through research and publication
that one's name becomes well-known and leads to speaking engage-
ments and publications that are well regarded nationally and internationally, the paths to recognition are many. In my own case, I received
a great deal of recognition in a number of ways, not the least of which
was being a well-known speaker and thus able to speak out on a
number of occasions.

In 1984, the APA gave me the Vestermark Award for outstanding
work in the area of education. My Vestermark speech was entitled,
"The Enigma of Stigma" (Fink, 1983). Again, it was one of those
memorable occasions that pushed my career in a specific direction.
The issue of stigma is the most critical factor in moving psychiatry out
of the shadows and into the mainstream of medicine. It has not yet
happened and may never happen because it is difficult to wipe out
stigma. The speech at the annual meeting of the APA was followed by
invitations from all over the country to speak on this topic. When I
became president of the American Psychiatric Association in 1989,
my theme for the year was "overcoming stigma." Allan Tasman,
Chairman of the Program Committee that year, and I edited a book
(Fink and Tasman, 1992) containing the best speeches and presentations on the topic. My name became inextricably related to the issue
of stigma.

For three years I had been the Chairman of the Council on
Education and Career Development and had been able to accomplish
a number of significant things. Because of my connections within the
academic world, I was challenged to start the PRITE (Psychiatry
Resident In-Training Examination) examination, which I did essentially on a dare. A recurrent statement made by people discussing the
issue of an inservice training exam for residents was that "psychiatry
could never get its act together to do such a thing." Within a year, I
had developed such an exam, and within three or four years we were
selling as many as 3,000 examinations out of my office. A group of
people came together once a year to write the exam. It was administered by Ohio State University, where the questions were validated. It
was a real educational instrument because it was new every year and

the exam, the questions, and a reference for each question were sent to the residents and their training directors annually. We also had a sense of daring that led to some foolishness. The examination was created with no compensation and was carried as an extra burden within my office. I had no liability insurance in the event someone sued us, and the program was becoming too large to be handled as a "mom and pop" operation. After a great deal of effort, I was able to induce the American College of Psychiatrists to take the program under its wing, and it has flourished so that today, almost 20 years later, it is a well-recognized examination taken by every resident in America and is being developed to be administered in a number of countries in Europe and South America. That project solidly sealed my reputation as a "doer." I began to be called upon to do a number of things. In addition, locally in Philadelphia, I gained recognition as a frequent commentator on television and radio and in the newspapers.

POLITICS AS USUAL

After I left Jefferson, I became Chairman of Psychiatry at Albert Einstein Medical Center and Medical Director of Philadelphia Psychiatric Center (now Belmont Center for Comprehensive Treatment), the private psychiatric hospital connected with Einstein, both in Philadelphia. The Public Relations Department of Einstein recognized my ability with the media and promoted it. With their help, I was able to gain recognition in the Philadelphia area, and, through my own efforts, working with the city and state Departments of Mental Health, I was able to participate in the political process. Obviously I enjoyed politics and I was moved to be involved in the political fray, regardless of where it was. People have quipped that I have been the president of every psychiatric organization possible (a slight exaggeration). I have participated in forums that were extremely important nationally in terms of public policy regarding mental health as well as general health. One day a colleague asked if I would allow my name to be on the ballot for president of the Philadelphia County Medical Society. I agreed with an inner sense that I couldn't possibly be elected. I hadn't risen through the ranks of the organization, and I didn't think I was well enough known to be elected. Nevertheless, because of my persona and the recognition that I had within the area, I was elected and became involved in medical as well as psychiatric issues in Southeastern Pennsylvania.

Each of my presidencies was characterized by an energy that made them special years in the histories of the respective organizations. Energy is important, and it is a quality that requires someone to set aside pettiness and work at the highest moral and ethical level (Fink, 1989). Using one's energy without trampling on people is an important part of growth in the academic sphere. The presidency of the County Medical Society opened many doors for me, and I began to move away from psychiatry and into the area of public activity. Philadelphia Mayor Edward Rendell appointed me to the Philadelphia Board of Health, and this appointment has allowed me to enter the area of power in avocational areas.

Two of my greatest areas of interest have been studying stigma against the mentally ill and the problem of violence in our society. Working in the area of violence has been more difficult than my work against stigma. My activism in the public arena has led to invitations to participate in meetings and committees and to work at problems with enormous energy, unpaid, and without much recognition. The difficulty here is that working without a portfolio and without appropriate entry into the field, one is often not taken seriously. This is another lesson in the area of politics. Credentials become very important. How does one claim a right to sit at the table? What is the basis on which one can be called an "expert" or get sufficient recognition to be included at the highest levels. The process is very complex and difficult.

Now in the last part of my career, I made a decision that I wanted to have an effect on the lives of thousands, if not millions, of children and I wanted to participate actively in an effort to address one of the most critical problems of the 90s. My position on the Board of Health led to my being named Chairman of the Youth Homicide Committee, a unique group in the City of Philadelphia that studies the homicides of children under the age of 22. It is not only an opportunity for epidemiological work, but it can lead to changes in public policy. My first such experience, which I have already discussed, was being on the School Board of Lower Merion Township. The idea that nine people could affect the lives of 10,000 children was a feeling of power which led to a great deal of satisfaction. Twenty-five years later and many successful jobs done, the reality that one hungers to be included is a pitfall that needs to be understood and recognized by psychiatrists aspiring to climb the ranks of organizations. The higher one goes, the more likely one is to be left out of the highest councils. It is inevitable that the rarified air at the top allows room for very few. Unawareness of one's hunger to be recognized, involved, and included may lead to a sense of unhappiness, if not despair.

Knowing one's limitations is also an important part of the political scene. Knowing where one is able to succeed, and making the right moves at the right time, are clearly essential parts of being successful. My inappropriate move at the beginning of my career at Jefferson is an example of what not to do. There are many examples along the way where the right timing leads to success—but the ability to know one's limitations is critical. Where is your presence appropriate and how much can you hope to achieve in the arena where so many are trying hard to reach the top of the hill? Most children have played "king of the hill," a game that is an appropriate metaphor for those who wish to participate in any administrative role, whether in the political arena, in the medical arena, or in institutional life. In looking back, I think the aphorism "It's not whether you win or lose, it's how you play the game" becomes a guidepost for people whose lives have been involved in supporting the growth and development of others, developing good programs, affecting the policies of the institution or system, and feeling fulfilled in one's career as a political activist.

CONCLUSION

There are some important lessons to be learned from my experience. If you want a career in organized medicine, you need the following qualities and conditions: 1) serendipity, 2) a good mentor, 3) the wish for recognition, 4) the search for inclusion, 5) the training for greater power, 6) charisma, 7) a willingness to work hard, 8) a sense of timing, 9) a willingness to take risks, 10) an ability to use opportunities.

Shakespeare said in *Julius Caesar*, "There comes a tide in the affairs of men which taken at the flood leads on to fortune." Clearly the ability to recognize high tide and the willingness to take an opportunity when it presents itself are critical for success as a leader. The excitement of success and the pain of failure are essential parts of such a career. In retrospect, it's been fabulous. Good luck to those of you who choose the path of organized medicine.

REFERENCES

Fink, P. J. (1983), The enigma of stigma and its relation to psychiatric education. *Psychiat. Ann.*, 13:669–690.

Fink, P. J. (1989), Presidential address: On being ethical in an unethical world. *Amer. J. Psychiat.*, 146:1097–1104.

Fink, P. J. & Tasman, A., ed., (1992), *Stigma and Mental Illness.* Washington, DC: American Psychiatric Press.

❋ 14 ❋

The Chinese Menu Track: One from Column A . . .

[HEALTH SERVICES AND POLICY]

Bernard S. Arons

Dr. Arons is director of the Center for Mental Health Services in the Substance Abuse and Mental Health Services Administration, United States Public Health Service. He has had a professional career dedicated to listening and responding to the concerns of people with mental illness and their families. A psychiatrist with expertise in financing mental health care, Dr. Arons has served in a variety of senior-level positions with the federal government. He also worked in a variety of positions at Saint Elizabeths Hospital. Dr. Arons is on the faculty of the Georgetown University School of Medicine and practices psychiatry at the Center for Mental Health, Inc., in Washington, DC. In 1989, selected as a legislative fellow in the U.S. Congress, Dr. Arons was an assistant in the office of Representative Pete Stark. In 1993, he served as an advisor on mental health issues to Tipper Gore's Office in the Office of the Vice President and was Chair of the Mental Health and Substance Abuse Working Group Cluster of the President's Task Force on National Health Care Reform. Dr. Arons is a graduate of Oberlin College and Case Western Reserve University School of Medicine.

Clinical practice, teaching, supervision, administration, policy development, psychotherapy, psychopharmacology – they all appeal to me. Ideally, I would like a job that combines them all. But that is a difficult job to find. It may not even exist. So I have tried to keep juggling a number of balls in the air at the same time, keeping up as best I can with some direct clinical work, some teaching, some administration. Many advised that it would have been more productive to pick a track

153

and stick with it. But for me, this approach has worked just fine. I certainly encourage medical students, psychiatric residents, and beginning psychiatrists to consider such a route—or such a balancing act, if you will. For me, it continues to be a stimulating and rewarding way to be a psychiatrist.

TRAINING

I started psychiatric training at Saint Elizabeths Hospital, at that time a federal public hospital that served as the "state" hospital for the District of Columbia with other federal responsibilities. There were long-term patients from the Virgin Islands and from American Indian reservations; there were "White House Cases," research units, forensic programs, and others. Although the hospital was bureaucratically under the National Institute of Mental Health (NIMH), there was little NIMH influence on the day-to-day operations of the hospital, which served individuals termed the poor, the involuntarily committed, the dangerous, the uninsured, the criminally charged, the noncitizens, the "no-fixed address." The training was exactly what I was looking for—it provided solid, intensive instruction in all aspects of psychiatry with excellent teachers in a public setting. No ivory tower was this experience. Included in my training experience was the night I got knocked out with a single punch by a young man seeking admission. (He was released by the ward psychiatrist the next day since he had "manipulated his way onto the ward.") More typical training experiences included individual, group, and family therapy with a range of people and in a variety of settings from hospital to university clinic to community organizations.

I did not really decide to go into psychiatry when I started training. I thought that a year or more of psychiatry would be helpful even if I ended up in internal medicine, emergency room medicine, pediatrics, or any of the other fields I was still contemplating. But as I got more deeply involved in understanding human behavior and the conditions that affect behavior, I discovered that no day was like the day before. The same diagnosis did not adequately reflect the unique situations presented by each new person with whom I worked. I came to feel quite comfortable with being a psychiatrist.

EARLY PROFESSIONAL EXPERIENCE

As I finished the training program, an opportunity arose for me to join the training faculty at the hospital. The next 14 years were professionally rewarding at an extraordinary level. I think there is nothing more pleasing than teaching in a clinical setting. Medical students, psychiatric residents, social work students, nursing students, psychology interns, high school and college students, lawyers, teachers, and others seemed hungry to understand better what happens to persons who have a mental illness and how best to treat them. My responsibilities changed, often at about the time I was getting tired of the previous tasks. Ward psychiatry, individual supervision, seminar teaching, community consultation, medical psychiatric consultation-liaison, long-term care, geriatric psychiatry were all part of the sprawling hospital complex. I slowly moved into some administrative areas and eventually headed up the effort to move the emphasis of clinical care from hospital to community. I ultimately became Chief Clinical Advisor, our name for medical director.

As Chief Clinical Advisor, I tried to model at the administrative level what we expected at the clinical level. I worked as part of an interdisciplinary team that combined psychology, nursing, social work, psychiatry, quality assurance, and other essential disciplines. We worked together to develop the rules and regulations, the policies and procedures that would make the clinical endeavor deliver the best treatment and rehabilitation services possible.

MORE ADMINISTRATION, POLICY, AND PLANNING

For several years I became immersed in assignments that can best be captured as more administration, including a heavy emphasis on policy and planning. I helped develop a plan to reorganize the system of care in the District of Columbia to better integrate and coordinate hospital and community services. Moving more into issues of financing mental health care, I developed an expertise in insurance coverage issues, Medicare, Medicaid, economic issues, and Federal policies and their influence on the delivery of mental health services.

I became intrigued with the notion that a change on the national policy level could have an impact on the ability of persons all over the country to access treatment for mental illness.

EXPERIENCE IN CONGRESS

I don't recall exactly what led me to apply for the LEGIS Fellows Program, but it was to have a tremendous impact on my life and my career. This is a program that allows federal government employees to have an opportunity to learn about Congress by working there for a period of time. There are similar programs for others who are not federal employees. After some training and seminars in the functions of the legislative branch of government, we were sent forth to maneuver ourselves into someone's office for some hands-on work. I guess if I lived on a lake or ocean, I would want to be sure to know how boats work. Living in Washington, DC, I figured it would be important to understand the local industry – the making of laws. And what they say is true: there are at least two things that should not be watched in the making – sausage and laws.

I was able to experience first-hand the activity swirling around Capitol Hill. The hearings, the committee meetings, the contacts with constituents, the analyses of policy "wonks," all work together to develop the laws governing our future. I had the privilege of working in the office of Fortney "Pete" Stark (D-CA), who remains one of the more active members of Congress in thinking about health issues, including mental health issues. The work involved areas far away from psychiatry. All House offices need to keep abreast of wide-ranging issues. I learned about sunglass standards as well as Medicare laws. The experience was truly unforgettable.

HEALTH CARE REFORM: TIPPER'S TOUCH

Clearly, the most remarkable experience of my professional career has been working with Tipper Gore on a variety of mental health issues. As an advisor on mental health to her office and as an assistant in the health care reform deliberation process, I had the privilege of meeting a tremendous number of dedicated persons who hope to develop a better system of care for individuals with mental illness. These people include consumers, family members, providers, administrators, policy makers, advocates, and politicians. Many would not be involved at all if not for the sincerity and persuasiveness of Mrs. Gore. Her decision to work on mental health issues while her husband served as vice-president provided a light, a direction, and the kind of leadership necessary to give people hope and encouragement.

I was pleased to have the opportunity to help her in this work. I know that not many psychiatrists will have the same kind of opportunity. Quite a number of psychiatrists, however, will have the opportunity to be available as an advisor to any one of a number of people in leadership positions who can make use of our unique perspective, if the advice is provided in a "user-friendly" way. School principals, mayors, state legislators, politicians and family members of politicians, and many others can become involved in societal issues related to mental health. I found that what I could provide was scientifically sound, clinically sensitive, policy-relevant, direct answers to difficult questions.

As the wife of the Vice President, Mrs. Gore has access to audiences whom I or any other psychiatrist could never hope to reach; she has access to policy makers who would view my input, if provided directly, as only self-serving professional protectionism. She is a symbol for many, many Americans who feel reassured that someone in her position cares about people with mental illness.

I had a number of varied responsibilities. I would help gather material for speeches. I would bring experts in for briefing sessions. I would comment on requests for appearances or talks. I would help produce briefing books on issues before major meetings were held. I would formulate policy options for her consideration. I would work with her staff to plan events, respond to citizens, attend to details. More informally, I would try to answer the many questions that have no good answers: Why is mental health treatment always given less coverage than other health treatment? What needs to be done to eliminate homelessness among people with mental illness? Why don't people take medications that are helping them? Why is there still such an intense stigma associated with mental illness?

Much of the work centered on the development of the Administration proposal for national health care reform. This chapter is not the place to analyze that episode in the ongoing evolution of the nation's health care. It is clear, however, that Tipper Gore was able to bring about some major accomplishments in that process. Attention was paid to mental health and substance abuse as part of health care reform at a level that had not been predicted. The eventual proposal and, more important, all alternative proposals included coverage for mental illness and substance abuse greater than the typical existing private insurance coverage. An educational process succeeded in bringing about a change in the attitude among policy makers toward coverage.

As a psychiatrist, I had the opportunity to be part of a policy development process that will, we hope, be a step in an ongoing process to assure greater access to treatment for individuals with mental illness.

THE CENTER FOR MENTAL HEALTH SERVICES: NATIONAL LEADERSHIP FOR SYSTEM CHANGE

I now serve as Director of the Center for Mental Health Services (CMHS), part of the Substance Abuse and Mental Health Services Administration in the U.S. Department of Health and Human Services. For me, this is a continuation and a furtherance of the work I have engaged in for my entire professional career. At CMHS we are trying to assure that the system of delivery of mental health services continues to improve the quality of life for people with mental illness and their families. We have come a long way as a nation. We no longer treat people with mental illness with neglect and blame. Yet, we still have a long way to go. Access to treatment is still unavailable to many. Stigma is still associated with mental illness and with those who provide treatment. Barriers to further work, to housing, and to other services stand in the way of people with mental illness returning to full membership in the community. In some situations, we still do not know what treatments and rehabilitation work best. In other situations, interventions we know can work are not available.

CMHS tries to improve this situation by supporting the infrastruc ture of care, pushing the system forward, and developing an efficient exchange of knowledge. We work with states and communities, with other federal agencies, with families and patients (who sometimes call themselves "consumers"), with professional organizations, and individual investigators. We fund special projects, pilot programs, larger scale demonstrations, technical assistance, and a number of surveys. We convene special task forces to provide direction and advice on issues of national policy.

CONCLUSION

The rewards of clinical care are unique. There is nothing as gratifying as working together with another human being to recover from difficulties or to learn to live constructively with those problems that can not be ended. The rewards of teaching are special. It is wonderful to convey knowledge, to inspire an interest in psychiatry, to enhance the skills of a younger physician. The rewards of administration, policy development, planning, and national leadership are somewhat more hazy, but equally wonderful. The immediate results are not always obvious. The gains are even slower than the sometimes slow progress of psychotherapy or response to medication. I view myself as privileged to be able to work in all these areas. I find it difficult to give up any. I tell myself, and I do believe, that each aspect of my professional work informs and supports each of the other aspects. I hope that this is, in fact, true.

RECOMMENDED READING

Bion, W. (1961), *Experience in Group*. London: Tavistock.

Buber, M. (1957), The William Alanson White memorial lectures, fourth series, *Psychiatry*, 20:95–129.

Caplan, G. (1970), *The Theory and Practice of Mental Health Consultation*. New York: Basic Books.

Frank, R. G., Goldman, H. H., & McGuire, T. G. (1992), A model mental health benefit in private health insurance. *Health Affairs*, 11(3):98–117.

Sharfstein, S. S. & Stoline, A. M. (1992), Reform issues for insuring mental health care. *Health Affairs*, 11(3):84–97.

※ 15 ※

Writing and Editing My Way Through Community Psychiatry, the Chronic Mentally Ill, Academia, and Managed Care

[EDITING AND WRITING]

John A. Talbott

Dr. Talbott is Professor and Chairman of the Department of Psychiatry at the University of Maryland School of Medicine and Director of the Institute of Psychiatry and Human Behavior at the University of Maryland Medical System in Baltimore, Maryland. He is the editor of *Psychiatric Services* (formerly *Hospital and Community Psychiatry*), President of the American Association of Chairmen of Departments of Psychiatry, Past President of the American Psychiatric Association and former Vice President of the American Board of Psychiatry and Neurology. Dr. Talbott has written or edited 20 books and over 200 articles dealing with mental health services, public policy, and the chronic mentally ill.

Some of my earliest memories are of my father's work table at home, with carefully laid out piles of chapters for books, papers for publication and slides for upcoming talks. My father would draft, write, revise, rewrite, endlessly. Much later I asked him how many times he revised each chapter, and the answer staggered me—it looked so easy and his writing was so elegant once it appeared in print. My father started writing in college, progressed to doing scientific papers as an academician, then became a part-time academician-editor of the "Green Journal" *Medicine*, and finally settled on his "last" career as the full-time editor of JAMA (introducing cover art to serious medical publishing for the first time) and director of all AMA specialty journals. He "retired" from the AMA to found a new journal in his subspecialty area (Seminars in Arthritis and Rheumatism) as well to edit The Merck Manual.

So it's not hard to guess where my interest in writing and editing came from. I, too, began early; in fact, I'm very proud of a "newspaper" I produced in grade school that presented the news of ancient Rome in a modern format. In preparatory school, I had as an English professor one of the most charismatic teachers and meticulous editors I have ever known—he taught me, then my father hired him to teach him, and one summer in college I took expository writing with him. In prep school, I coedited the monthly school newspaper, the last issue of which had a spiced-up and obviously doctored opinion survey of "best" this and "most" that, which resulted in an emergency faculty meeting where my coeditor and I came a whisker's length from expulsion. Harvard, however, had a place for trouble-makers like me—the Lampoon, where I spent endless hours writing, selling advertisements, editing, cooking, and pasting up copy. Even in medical school I realized there was fun to be had. I wrote a silly guide to New York for incoming students and edited what had become a rather traditional yearbook, spending several hilarious weeks with a group of largely ex-Lampoon classmates captioning what we thought were ridiculous photos of the faculty and students.

But I've jumped ahead of myself, for four years before I had had to make a critical decision: graduate school in English or medical school. At this point, the real world intruded—I realized that eventually I had to earn a living, and I suddenly panicked at the thought of academic poverty.

MORE EDUCATION

I had a very exciting medicine internship at Rochester, but it didn't leave much time for contemplative thinking. My primary achievements included resuscitating one man more times than a human being should have to endure and resuscitating more patients than any other house officer in sight.

But it was residency that started me on what I now see as an interesting career path. When I returned to Columbia, my betters concluded that I knew the mother ship rather well already and assigned me, for my first two months, to Rockland State Hospital, far from Manhattan's charms and glitter. I met the superintendent twice, once when he welcomed me and gave me a key to the wards and again when I left. He and pretty nearly everybody else in authority left me alone. Well, that's charitable – they did heaven knows what, but it was neither supervision nor teaching. Which was okay with me. I read my Ernest Jones's (1953–57) *The Life and Work of Sigmund Freud* on the bus to and from Orangeburg, sat in my stiflingly hot office waiting for relatives to show up on weekends, and madly instituted "new programs" for what felt like 180 patients. I started several patients who had been tossing emboli on anticoagulants; I started group therapy for all those who would participate; and I reassessed everyone's diagnosis and medication, much to the annoyance of the pharmacy ("We don't carry that") and nursing staff ("But Mr. Jones has always got Thorazine once a day"). I was depressed and lonely, but for some reason I loved it; the state hospital was a sort of frontier and the patients its fascinating inhabitants.

COMMUNITY PSYCHIATRY

Later in residency I was entranced with what was called "community psychiatry" at the New York State Psychiatric Institute. This community psychiatry was really an early attempt to treat patients from subcatchment areas with small teams, *but only as inpatients.* When I graduated, I continued on the Community Unit half-time and also got a grant to work half-time in the Outpatient Department and the Visiting Nurse Service and as liaison between the two (see MacKinnon, Talbott, and Holloway, 1969). Thus, I started "doing community psychiatry" before I had a term for it.

Fate, or at least the war in Viet Nam, intervened at this point, and I was drafted. While my wife and I debated moving to Switzerland, Sweden, or Canada (where my family had come from), I was convinced by my chairman, Larry Kolb, and the most influential community psychiatry researcher in the Department, Ernie Gruenberg, that I'd learn much more community psychiatry in the Army than at Columbia. And they were right, at least for me. For both at Fort Bragg and in Viet Nam, I found myself going out "into the field" to practice "command consultation," the Army's version of community consultation (Talbott, 1969). As I had in my Visiting Nurse home care project in New York, I liked training and consulting to other professionals and administrators, liked doing it where it was, and felt that sitting in the clinic was boring. Especially in Viet Nam, I fought off boredom and depression by reading and writing and had made nine contributions to the literature after two years' service. Viet Nam was a horrible experience, politically and emotionally, but it was wonderful from the standpoint of professional autonomy, personal assessment, and psychiatric learning.

I had been approached by Robert Michels, a colleague from Columbia then at St. Luke's Hospital in New York, about joining him after my discharge from military service to start a Consultation/Liaison Division. The NIMH money didn't come through, however, and this quirk of fate again changed my career. For Bob felt some obligation to find me something else, and when a half-time position opened up in, of all places, community psychiatry, I took it. I should mention that in the interim I had tried my hand at full-time solo private practice in a professional building and found it more lonely and isolative than either Rockland State or Viet Nam. I also should mention that even then I dreamt of dividing up the whole country by the number of psychiatrists and having each assume total care of the resultant population; I just wanted one housing project in New York. It's eerie how capitation and modern public psychiatry have made my dream a real possibility.

In those heady times, the 60s, community psychiatry meant everything nontraditional; community consultation to the police (Talbott and Talbott, 1971), making films on single-room occupancy hotel living for deinstitutionalized state hospital patients, and crisis intervention using para- and other professionals. For me, it also meant being heavily involved in the beginning and rebirth of Viet Nam Veterans Against the War, and I began to see the importance of grass-roots political action. Together with our nextdoor neighbors, my wife and I started a 24-hour-a-day reading of the names of the Viet Nam war dead at Riverside Church. This also turned into a series of lessons on administration: from how to establish telephone-trees to how to handle bomb and kidnapping threats; from how to get publicity to how to set up an office with "day ladies" to coordinate each day's readers, who included Leonard Bernstein and Leontine Price, courtesy of our New York Philharmonic director-neighbor, and Craig Claiborne and Mrs. Harrison Salisbury, courtesy of front-page coverage in the *New York Times*. I became the Readings' spokesperson and did a lot of interviews; this was invaluable in teaching me how to give a 20-second sound bite or one-paragraph answer.

AN ABRUPT CHANGE OF CAREER

One day, however, I was told by my ultimate boss at St. Luke's that I was no longer needed. The reason he gave was that I "hadn't done enough," at which my former chairman at Columbia snorted and said "rather too much, I'd say." Indeed, there were two reasons. First, while the Viet Nam Memorial Reading was a protest, it would be hard to say it was improper or disrespectful. Knowing that my boss's politics did not include opposition to the war, I had embarrassed him into appearing to read some names of the war dead. Second, I had apparently also outraged the hospital's conservative administration and board by signing a full-page statement in two New York newspapers protesting the war.

To top it off, in line with the way things were done in those days, some self-designated "community representatives," backed by some self-styled "radical psychiatrists," held a "sit-in" in the Division of Community Psychiatry offices to protest St. Luke's sluggish response to a rash of adolescent deaths from heroin overdoses in nearby Harlem. The "representatives" had originally come to our offices, which were located in an apartment building outside the hospital walls, probably because they (mistakenly) thought that we in Community Psychiatry treated drug abuse or because they thought "community" meant answerable to them (these were the "power to the people" days after all). Unfortunately, our offices were also the only easily occupiable hospital target. Anyway, the "community" representatives demanded more drug treatment. I huddled with the hospital's administration and got a nonanswer, but I was able to dig up an old and rejected application to the NIMH for a drug abuse treatment program written by the group in psychiatry that *was* responsible for treating drug abuse. Sure enough, when the "community" occupied our offices, there the application was in my office. Cleverly, they confronted us with the fact that St. Luke's *had* recognized the problem and demanded the hospital fund the program itself. I became a negotiator between the hospital and the "representatives," in retrospect, a grave mistake, since the "representatives" certainly didn't trust me and once I began practicing shuttle diplomacy, the hospital no longer saw me as one of theirs. Reciprocally, I had sympathy for the "community's" plight but not their "representatives'" style (Huey Newton-type gun belts), rhetoric, or manner and slowly lost respect for the hospital's decision-making ability and creativity. I suspect the hospital never truly believed that I was not a traitor for leaving the grant in my very vulnerable office. Sometime later, I attempted a feeble and naive retaliation by writing an article (Talbott, 1974) about the content of the newsletter (*Radical Psychiatry*) some of those involved in the "sit-in" wrote for; I think the shots fell dreadfully short. In retrospect, though, I had learned a lot: that a "community psychiatry" that didn't deliver care to the seriously ill but did a lot of community consultation and education had misplaced values, that you should be a mediator only if you were so chosen by both parties and well paid for it, and that a lot of silliness was perpetrated in the name of "community action" then.

But there I was, looking for a job. "Community psychiatry" positions were not numerous, but New York's state hospitals were 16 years into deinstitutionalization and intriguing possibilities appeared.

STATE HOSPITAL PSYCHIATRY

I put together a job—one half-time working at Columbia on educational programs, largely in video, for the state hospital system and the other half-time in a related job, serving on a multidisciplinary "team" that was supposed to train "chronic" state hospital inpatient employees about moving patients and services into the "community" (Talbott et al., 1973). The training team was a wonderful group where, despite the vogue at the time for "role-blurring," professional expertise was valued. We had fun between and among ourselves. The problems came in dealing with our "customers." In one hospital, the superintendent greeted me warmly and said how much he respected me and how he hoped I'd have an impact on his staff. But, after he introduced me to the hospital's medical staff, without warning he quickly left the room. Just as quickly, I figured out that without his backing I might as well go back to Manhattan. Not all folks in the state hospital system were quite so scared, however, and we made some progress. But I couldn't help but feel that, if only I could grab some of that superintendent's power, given what I knew, I could change things.

At this point, a job opened up as Deputy Director at one of the then-fragmented parts of Manhattan State Hospital, which had a very loose relationship with Columbia. I sought the advice of my former chairman, and he suggested I take it, but only if I could also become the Director of Education and Training. He offered to "up" his involvement with the hospital. So it came to pass that Lawrence C. Kolb, one of the most respected men in psychiatry, assigned himself as the first faculty member and the star junior resident at Columbia, Stuart Yudofsky (now chair at Baylor and coeditor with Bob Hales and myself of the *APPI Textbook of Psychiatry*) as the first trainee, to begin the affiliated rotation by spending two months at Manhattan State.

I spent three years more on Ward's Island, culminating as Director (Superintendent) at part of the hospital (Dunlap). There, our motto was, "At Dunlap, it can be done," referring to the most common resistance we encountered to any change. We would propose, for instance, to make the wards coed and would be told it "couldn't be done." I resolved to keep a diary at Dunlap chronicling my attempted changes and resistances and, while unable to sustain its daily recording, had enough after a while to think about writing up my experience in the context of state hospital change and deinstitutionalization (Talbott, 1978a).

I should mention at this point that what often kept me positively involved in situations that could have been overwhelmingly frustrating, whether in Viet Nam, at St Luke's, or at Manhattan State, was my dedication of certain off-hours to writing. On my return to the United States from Viet Nam, I became involved in our APA District Branch newsletter (actually I had written an article from Viet Nam while there). The then-editor was an old mentor from Columbia who encouraged my foray into what was my first go at medical journalism. I was also writing and editing books as well as contributing to journals.

But despite these attempts to better understand the systems I was working in and communicate my understanding to others, I was getting exhausted by the battles. I returned to my psychiatric father and by now ex-chairman, Larry Kolb, for advice. For once he wasn't understanding. He had left Columbia to become New York's State Commissioner of Mental Health and, I suspect, saw my frustration and wish to get out as abandonment, saying he needed me where I was. I, however, told him, I wasn't sure that I, with all my book knowledge and credentials (by then I was active in the APA certification process in Administrative Psychiatry), was doing any better a job than the most poorly respected of directors. I also harbored the thought that maybe I needed to move to the national scene, where I could finally have an impact.

By now, even I saw this flight elsewhere as a familiar theme. I had left St. Luke's, the recipient of crude deinstitutionalization, to better shape good community care for discharged state hospital patients by educating staff. I had left the state hospital training team because I felt I couldn't truly do this by persuasion but needed direct line authority. And I left line authority for a national pulpit because I thought that only that would work.

ON TO THE CHRONIC MENTALLY ILL

Bob Michels, who had engineered my first post-Viet Nam job, now offered me a position at Cornell. We originally talked about the need for the New York Hospital to demolish the old Payne-Whitney building and move its programs outside while a new building was constructed. He thought that would be an interesting challenge for me. (For the sake of history, I must reveal that this was 1975, and now, 21 years later, just such a series of events is underway.) Other tasks, however, loomed, and they seemed so manageable after Manhattan State. It became clear to me that whatever my salary source, a concentration on either hospital or community care alone was insufficient and a focus on the entire service system was necessary.

In 1978, the APA held the "Key Conference," to which I was sent by my APA district branch, in part to present a call to action about the chronic mentally ill, who were then flooding Manhattan's emergency rooms. In time, the APA sponsored a conference devoted to the problem and out of it a series of publications (Talbott, 1978b) and actions emerged. I became the chair of the APA's Committee on the Chronic Mentally Ill and parallel to this was working my way up from District Branch representative to the APA Assembly to APA Area Trustee to APA President. All the while, however, I was actively advocating for better care and treatment of the chronically ill.

During this period, I also became the first APA member-editor of *Hospital & Community Psychiatry*, a journal I had often published in and reviewed for and on whose Editorial Board Committee I had served. This move had an interesting echo; for, when I was at Manhattan State I had been active in editing the *Psychiatric Quarterly*, a journal originally intended for New York State hospital superintendents. Thus, I had moved both professionally and editorially from hospital to hospital *and* community and, as of this writing, to service systems in my current position, a journey that roughly paralleled the journal's name change from *Mental Hospitals* to *Hospital and Community Psychiatry* to *Psychiatric Services*.

SERVICE SYSTEMS

One day, my colleague and (on paper) subordinate Allen Frances told me he had just looked at the Chair at Maryland, and while it wasn't for him it was ideal for me. After I recovered from this narcissistic blow, I decided to take a look.

He was right. The University of Maryland had three intriguing and unique features for a Department of Psychiatry (Talbott and Robinowitz, 1986). It was strong clinically, with an excellent and balanced array of services and affiliated relations with private and public facilities; it had the world's most outstanding schizophrenia research center, with scientists ranging from neurochemists to sociologists; and it had an award-winning relationship with the state that had resulted in dozens of Maryland-trained psychiatrists entering the public system. The administrative challenge—and administration had always fascinated me (Talbott and Kaplan, 1983; Talbott, Hales, and Keill

1992) – was to establish a true service system (Talbott, 1983) that could take on a growing patient responsibility.

In the 10 years I've been at Maryland we've grown phenomenally, going from $2 million in outside grants and contracts to $20 million, from a residency and two fellowships to five more fellowships; and we've established a brand new research endeavor on campus with our Center for Mental Health Services Research, which is equal in fire-power to our basic schizophrenia research center. Its creation also accelerated my interest in financing (Talbott and Sharfstein, 1986). In addition, we've moved closer to having a truly complete service system, with all possible product and service lines available to serve all patients, including those who were traditionally indemnity-funded and those publicly supported.

MANAGED CARE

At present, we have not only the usual traditional inpatient services targeted to disease and age specific populations, but a very short ("Managed Care") unit; the usual outpatient clinics and satellites serving patients reimbursed by various sources, including contracts, but also a presence in our primary-care satellites and off-site group practice offices; the traditional day hospitals and psychosocial programs, again targeted to age and disease, but also community care teams for the homeless and dually diagnosed, as well as case management; and not only traditional emergency services but a new university urgent care center that performs assessment, triage, referral, crisis management, and crisis treatment – all this supported and studied by our mental health services research faculty (Talbott, 1987).

As I stated earlier, I have also moved editorially with the flow over time, sensing that the name of the journal I edit would better describe our current environment if it were entitled *Psychiatric Services*, rather than being bound to institutional settings. And, in my work with the Association of Chairmen of Psychiatry, my committee, which 10 years ago was established to concentrate on faculty practice plan and reimbursement, now deals almost exclusively with managed care issues.

WHAT TO MAKE OF ALL THIS

I was asked by the editor of this book to dispense some advice to our colleagues contemplating career decisions or changes. This is especially difficult for me since I'm really not sure how much writing and editing can be taught, and I'm not really sure how I got where I am, despite my account here.

Indeed, a number of years ago, a faculty colleague remarked to a mutual friend that I was an opportunist. While I was wounded then to hear this, now I consider it to be a very desirable trait. Who knows what the future of psychiatry is, but being there when the opportunity arises is certainly preferable to being shaped by uncontrollable forces.

As a corollary, I do have one regret, but that is trivial in a life where everything else turned out okay. Would I could do it over again, I'd have taken my primary mentor's advice and gone to the NIMH following residency, not to avoid Viet Nam, but to have had that experience and scientific acumen in my data set.

Speaking of mentors, they were of immense importance to me. Sure, I have a love of writing and editing that is either genetic or close to it. But without the model of my father, the inspiration of my prep school English teacher, the encouragement of my district branch bulletin editor, and the guidance of my former chairman, I don't think I'd be where I am today.

Finally, somehow I figured out what I did well and what I liked, and often they were identical. Likewise what I did poorly and what I disliked were also usually linked. I'm not saying I don't do a lot of things that are difficult, boring, or painful, but the joy I get from writing or editing or starting up a new program or service far outweighs the nonsense involved.

In the final analysis, I think you've got to take risks and see if they pay off. If they do, it makes all the sweat and stress doubly sweet.

REFERENCES

Jones, E. (1953–57), The Life and Work of Sigmund Freud, Vols. I-III, New York: Basic Books.

MacKinnon, R., Talbott, J. A., & Holloway, B. (1969), Psychiatric care through home nursing services. In: Current Psychiatric Therapies, ed. J. H. Masserman, New York: Grune & Stratton, pp. 218–223.

Talbott, J. A. (1969), Community psychiatry in the army: History, practice and applications to civilian psychiatry. J. Amer. Med.

Assn., 210:1233–1237.

Talbott, J. A. (1974), Radical psychiatry: An examination of issues raised in *The Radical Therapist. Amer. J. Psychiat.*, 131:121–128.

Talbott, J. A. (1978a), *The Death of the Asylum: A Critical Study of State Hospital Management, Services and Care.* New York: Grune & Stratton.

Talbott, J. A. (1978b), *The Chronic Mental Patient: Problems, Solutions and Recommendations for a Public Policy.* Washington, DC: American Psychiatric Association.

Talbott, J. A. (1983), *Unified Mental Health Systems: Utopia Unrealized.* San Francisco: Jossey Bass.

Talbott, J. A. (1987), Economic aspects of schizophrenia. Guest Editor. *Psychiat. Annals*, 17:9.

Talbott, J. A., Hales, R. E., & Keill, S. L. (1992), *Textbook of Administrative Psychiatry.* Washington, DC: American Psychiatric Press.

Talbott, J. A. & Kaplan, S. R. (1983), *Psychiatric Administration: A Comprehensive Text for the Clinician-Executive.* New York: Grune & Stratton.

Talbott, J. A. & Robinowitz, C. (1986), *Working Together: State-University Collaboration in Mental Health.* Washington, DC: American Psychiatric Press.

Talbott, J. A., Ross, A. M., Skerrett, A. F., Curry, M. D., Marcus, S. I., Theodorou, H., & Smith, B. J. (1973), The paraprofessional teaches the professional. *Amer. J. Psychiat.*, 130:805–808.

Talbott, J. A. & Sharfstein, S. S. (1986), A proposal for future funding of chronic and episodic mental illness. *Hosp. & Comm. Psychiat.*, 37:1126–1130.

Talbott, J. A. & Talbott, S. W. (1971), Training police in community relations and urban problems. *Amer. J. Psychiat.*, 127:894–900.

❊ 16 ❊

On Being an Entrepreneur

[ENTREPRENEURISM]

Kenneth A. Kessler

Dr. Kessler is the founder and CEO of American Psych Systems, an integrated regional behavioral healthcare delivery system. He is also the founder and former CEO of American Psych Management, now part of Value Behavioral Health. After training at the University of Pennsylvania, Dr.Kessler established a psychopharmacology clinic in 1974, served as Chief of Psychopharmacology and Director of the Attending Unit at the Psychiatric Institute of Washington, and was Director of Outpatient Services of the Metropolitan Psychiatric Group. Dr. Kessler has written numerous articles and book chapters in the field of psychiatry.

WHY BECOME AN ENTREPRENEUR?

Two Bad Reasons

In the 1980s, American industry began downsizing to meet global competition. One of the first victims of this change was the notion that working for a large corporation offered long-term job security. About the same time, studies were published showing that most of this country's new jobs were being created by rapidly growing small companies. The combination of these two developments helped to glamorize people who started new businesses. In the late 1980s, entrepreneurship began to be seen as a tonic to restore the vitality of the nation's economy. Entrepreneurs were seen, not as Mao's "running dogs of capitalism," but as the cultural heroes of the 90s. Those of us whose formative experience was in the 1960s could not help but wonder what a difference a couple of decades can make. Social trendiness, however, is not a good reason to start a business. The journey is too strenuous and the road too long for one to choose to be an entrepreneur simply because it's in fashion.

Another compelling reason not to become an entrepreneur is to make a lot of money, or what is known as wealth generation. To start with, something like 90% of all new businesses fail. The combination of the long odds against success and the enormous personal embarrassment of failing in public suggests that the Irish Lottery may be a more prudent avenue for those seeking a quick road to riches. This is not to say that money is irrelevant. Unlike some entrepreneurs, who see money only as a "scorecard" by which to measure success, I believe that a nice payday is an important ingredient in making the equation work. Entrepreneurs may not start businesses to get rich, but one would be hard put to justify the sacrifice and risk if there were not a substantial economic reward for success.

One Good Reason

If being a cultural hero and achieving wealth is not a good reason to become an entrepreneur, what is? For me, the answer was captured by a remark the film director John Huston made. A reporter asked Huston why he had returned in his 70s to acting after moving up the ladder from working in a circus to being a senior statesman of the movie business. Huston replied, "Why, to stay interested, of course. What other reason is there to do anything?" Huston's remark answered the metaphysical question that college students traditionally spend their sophomore year wrestling with: what is it all about? John Huston had offered a stunningly simple answer that worked for me. What it's really about is staying interested. And I find the challenges of starting a business about as interesting as it gets.

The rest of the explanation of why I became an entrepreneur has to do with giving up the idea that one career could be so fulfilling that it could keep me interested for a lifetime. Robert Jay Lifton (1971) helped to legitimize the notion that changing careers did not mean that I had chosen badly the first time. It helped me to understand that one job was unlikely to meet my need for stimulation and satisfaction over a 35-year career.

The reason I became an entrepreneur, then, was that starting a business interested me. It was an important enough undertaking to give me a sense of mission, a feeling that I was doing something more than just earning a living. I also like the tempo and variety of challenges involved in starting a business. Every day is unlike the day before. Things happen too quickly to allow one to get into a routine, let alone a rut. I found the clinical practice of psychiatry enormously gratifying, but, after 10 years, I had begun to cruise on autopilot. I knew that I would not stay interested for another 25 years and worried that if I waited too long I would get stuck. The question for me became: what was I prepared to do about it? I had no interest in being retooled as a lawyer or an architect. A more logical choice was to build on the skills I already had, but to use them in a different way that offered new challenges. This led me to think of starting a business in the field of mental health care.

STARTING AMERICAN PSYCH MANAGEMENT (APM)

Cost Containment, Not Hospitals

Thus 10 years into my medical career, I was thinking about starting a business. The logical business to start would have been a psychiatric hospital, but I had stopped believing in them. Two formative experiences had changed my thinking about psychiatric hospitals. The first was running a psychopharmacology clinic from 1974 to 1984. By the clinic's third year of operations, we had reduced the hospital admission rate for approximately 120 affectively disordered patients from 40 admits annually to one a year. While the central role of medications in managing serious mental illness is now firmly established, in the early 70s medication was viewed by the profession as an unproven modality that merely "suppressed symptoms." The clinic showed that a medical model could avoid many, if not most, psychiatric hospitalizations. As a result, psychiatric hospitals began to take on a negative valance for me. The other significant event was that I served on the finance committee of a large private psychiatric hospital. This experience convinced me that there was a great deal of fat in employers' mental health costs. The combination of these two experiences led me to conclude that I did not want to run a psychiatric hospital because I no longer believed in the hospital's mission. Further, I began to believe that there was an interesting opportunity in helping employers provide a more cost-effective mental health benefit. The question was, was I ready to take the plunge?

Bring Your Spouse Along

Early in the process, I began to discuss the possibility of starting a business with my wife. Since my career was going well, my wife, not surprisingly, questioned the wisdom of changing directions. I held a couple of salaried positions, my outpatient practice had a waiting list, I had published a number of articles in refereed journals, and I was poised to coast into a contented middle-age. My wife tried to dissuade me by dismissing my plan as a "midlife crisis," a concept that was elastic enough to cover most problems between adolescence and senescence. While my wife may or may not have made the correct diagnosis, I eventually persuaded her that the right treatment was for me to scratch the itch, rather than to analyze why I had it.

For any married person contemplating starting a business, I can't recommend strongly enough the wisdom of getting your spouse's buy-in. Things rarely go as planned, and most of the surprises are unwelcome. When you're awake at 2 AM thinking about losing the financial foundation for your comfortable, middle-class life, it helps to have someone to talk to who isn't going to remind you that she thought it was a bad idea from the start. In fact, it helps to have at least several people you can talk to, since eventually even your spouse gets bored with your obsession and wants to talk about such distractions as the children and her career.

Good Advice from a Successful Entrepreneur

There are problems and challenges common to most business startups, and learning what to expect from others who've already done it is good preparation. One of the founders of a national psychiatric hospital company gave me some particularly helpful advice. He noted that I had done well without ever having fully committed myself. As he put it, "You've always juggled at least three balls at a time." His first recommendation, therefore, was to put all other activities aside and devote myself wholly to this undertaking. This simple advice was profoundly helpful. It's hard to overestimate the intensity and commitment required to launch a business. Serving on boards, managing personal investments, and even such hobbies as photography and cooking all got squeezed out of my life early in the process. Starting a business can best be described as an all-consuming beast that encompasses the worst features of a severe addiction and a demanding mistress. The second piece of advice he offered was that a new business starts with sales, not with operations. Since I'd never seen myself as a gifted salesman and was uncomfortable with public speaking, this unwelcome insight was an early test of my resolve. Once I came to terms with it, I enrolled in a course for advanced selling techniques and joined Toastmasters, a self-help group that helps people become more effective public speakers.

Have a Business Plan

I had decided to start a business. The next challenge was to write a business plan outlining how the company would work. Writing a business plan is a tedious exercise that many entrepreneurs avoid. This is a big mistake, and one that probably dooms many startups to failure. Until you can write out what your product or service is, whom you are selling to, how much you will get paid, where the profit will come from, and how you are going to deliver the service, you don't understand your business and aren't ready to start. Starting a business without a plan is akin to trying to hit a bullseye through Brownian movement: you may get there, but it's not a good bet. In developing a business plan, the would-be entrepreneur is forced to think through solutions to problems that will become apparent later. If you can't think of good solutions to these problems, it may mean that there are no good answers. If that's true, it's better to know the bad news sooner rather than later.

Part of a business plan is making financial projections. While the first several cuts may be a little capricious and a lot arbitrary, the entrepreneur needs progressively to refine his assumptions. This exercise is likely to uncover serious flaws in the plan. Most entrepreneurs project early profitability on the basis of above-market pricing and underestimating operating expenses. Almost invariably, market prices are lower, costs are higher, and greater volume is needed to become profitable.

Dream Realistically

The business plan I developed in 1983 forecast a company that would achieve annual sales of $100 million by 1990. At the time I made it, this forecast seemed wildly grandiose since carving out mental health from employer indemnity insurance plans had, to my knowledge, never been done. (I subsequently learned that a startup company had carved out mental health benefits for municipal employees in Southern California.) The idea of building a national business based on the employer's carve out (ECO) becoming a mainstream product—and projecting that an as yet unborn company would achieve a 10% marketshare of a $1 billion industry—seemed hopelessly naive. While on the speaking circuit two years later, I met a prominent mental health care analyst. I was surprised to learn that she envisioned the ECO's becoming a billion dollar industry within five years. At the time, I thought that her naivete was even more dangerous than mine, since I had to be militantly optimistic to take the plunge, while she was being paid to be skeptical about people like me. This Cassandra proved right, however; about five years later the ECO emerged as a mainstream product, and the industry had grown to $1 billion in annual sales. Two years after that, APM passed the $100 million mark. So much for hopelessly naive forecasts. Without a healthy dose of optimism, no business would ever be launched.

You Can't Go Home

Having written a business plan, been encouraged by successful entrepreneurs, won my wife's support, and overcome my reluctance to be retooled as a salesman, I now had to "just do it." I needed to cross my personal Rubicon by committing to a start date when I would begin working on the business half-time. I had an intuitive sense that I could pull it off if I climbed far enough out on a limb so that there was no graceful way to come back. In reducing my professional activities to 15–20 hours a week and shutting off all new referrals, I was committing myself to an irrevocable life-change. With the loss of my referral base, I did not expect to reestablish a clinical practice in Washington, DC if the business failed. The market was becoming oversupplied, and the prospect of starting over in the same city 12 years after the first launch was unappealing. I developed a contingency plan that, if the business failed, the family would relocate to Naples, on the West Coast of Florida. Naples seemed to be an undersupplied but growing market that was ready made for people wanting to leave their past behind and start over. I shared this plan with my wife, and over time we both grew more comfortable with the idea. Since I don't enjoy high humidity, I had all the more reason to make the business a success.

Learning Who Your Customer Really Is

While the business plan called for carving out mental health benefits from employer indemnity plans, my experience in meeting with employers proved disappointing. The first problem was that I rarely got to meet employers. Once I started selling a product, I was just another salesman fighting for a benefit manager's time. The first challenge, therefore, was getting past the secretary. The course I had taken in advanced salesmanship taught me how to enlist the secretary as an ally in getting air time with her boss. Having spent months overcoming this obstacle, I was profoundly disappointed when I learned that in 1983 most employers did not have a clue as to what they were spending for mental health and had no interest in finding out. When I explained that mental health costs were growing rapidly and that there were more efficient ways of managing the benefit, most employers responded that, if they had a problem, their insurance carrier would manage it for them. The critical role played by insurance carriers was driven home by a benefit manager who explained that while he might be interested in using APM's services, he had no interest in having APM become his "four hundred and first vendor." He urged me to establish a supplier relationship with his insurance carrier, which would sell our service to him.

This suggestion led me to begin meeting with insurance carriers. Through networking and calling in years' worth of favors, I was able to arrange a high-level meeting with senior executives of one of the country's largest carriers. The meeting educated me to the realities of an insurance carrier's relationship with its clients. The eyes of my audience glazed over when I discussed how the mental heath benefit could be managed more effectively. But when I talked about managed mental health care as a hot new element in the managed care continuum, my audience leaned forward and listened attentively. Afterwards I asked my host what I should make of these observations. He explained that most insurance carriers had long ago lost interest in actually insuring health care and that the majority of their revenues came from processing claims. Claims paying was charged to employers as a percentage of the total dollar value of the claims processed. I observed that it might not be in the short-term interest of an insurance carrier to reduce the dollar value of claims paid but that it could be in its interest to be perceived as laboring diligently on behalf of employers by trying new cost-containment programs (provided they didn't succeed too much). My host looked at me with a knowing grin, which seemed to say, "You're not as dumb as I first thought."

Otherwise Known as a Strategic Charge to the Rear

I had learned some interesting lessons in my first six months of trying to sell the ECO. The first lesson was that most employers did not know what they were spending for mental health and had no interest in finding out. The second was that insurance carriers had a financial disincentive to implement real cost containment. The third lesson was that psychiatric hospitals and organizations representing mental health professionals wanted to block the inroads of managed care and were quick to exaggerate the potential problems of any cost containment program. Finally, I had climbed out to the end of a limb in a very public way and the possibility of falling off was becoming a concern. This led me to one of many crossroads on the journey to starting APM. In trying to sell a capitated mental health benefit to employers, I had chosen a product that nobody wanted to buy and that influential players—such as insurance carriers and psychiatric hospitals—were actively hostile to. Confronting these realities was very disappointing and a tad discouraging.

Entrepreneurs must be resilient by nature and able to be reinvigorated by finding the lesson behind each new setback. Freud observed that a mother's first-born son never knows true despair. If that's true, being a first-born son is very helpful in launching a business. Rather than packing our bags for Naples, I did a quick 180° turn in an effort to get APM launched in the remaining six months before our funds ran out. The 180° turn was to change my strategy from selling to employers, at least for the time being, and to focus on selling to HMOs. The result of this strategic charge to the rear was that by the 12th month of a 12-month window, I closed two contracts. This episode has a lesson in it for all would be entrepreneurs. You probably don't know what your product *really* is or what your primary market will turn out to be until you start selling. If you're really committed and can't climb back, you will keep zigging and zagging until you improvise your way into a sale. And a sale is the beginning of a business. Without it, all you have is unused capacity. Actually getting into business, albeit at a very modest level, took APM past the second critical landmark in its birth. We were an operating business, rather than a concept in my mind.

Early APM

The early days of APM were, in many ways, the most satisfying for me. Without a track record or adequate capitalization, we were unable to attract an experienced management team, with the exception of our medical director. We were forced to rely on people with youth, energy, and drive. The enthusiasm of this team was remarkable, and its commitment still inspires me. The first APM employee was my Administrative Assistant. I interviewed a series of women who came properly attired and had college degrees from respectable universities. When I asked how they felt being the face of the company while I was out, however, most of them turned a paler shade of pale. When asked this litmus question, the winning candidate answered, "This sounds like we're going to have a lot of fun." Our first proposal writer was an unemployed college graduate with a degree in philosophy. Since GE and GM weren't screaming for more philosophers to join their management teams, we were able to hire him for an embarrassingly modest amount. Both of these people had the energy and drive to keep rising through the ranks. Having started for salaries in the teens, both eventually moved on to other companies, where they are now making six-figure incomes.

One early APMer whom I recently bumped into told me, with a degree of wistfulness, that it wasn't until after she left APM that she realized what a unique experience it had been. She doubted that she would ever again work with as bright and motivated a group of people as she had at APM. This motivation came across in manys ways. One that stands out 10 years later is the July 4 weekend of 1986. We had recently learned of a request for proposal (RFP) for a large capitated mental health contract that was about to be let by the Department of Defense. We found out late and were playing catch-up. In order to complete a first draft of an RFP response and to do our pricing, most of the company came in to work through the holiday weekend. Unfortunately, we were not able to have the building's air conditioning turned on. Since it was a hot day and the windows couldn't be opened, the work environment quickly deteriorated. By the third day, it was so uncomfortable that some people closed their doors and worked in their underwear. By the end of the weekend, we had our first draft and our first cut at pricing. No one complained or asked for overtime. In the early days, we saw ourselves as an elite team operating at the cutting edge, inventing the business as we went. It was an intense experience that enabled us to commit ourselves in a way that rarely happens in most work environments.

Growing Pains

While those were the times I enjoyed the most, they could not go on indefinitely. As the managed behavioral health care business became an industry, we needed to professionalize. Many of the people whose energy and drive launched APM did not adapt well to organizational structure. I tried to protect them, but over time many no longer fit in and chose to move on. In this stage of APM's development, the excitement and creativity of the first couple of years gave way to the need to become profitable and to maintain a leadership position in a rapidly growing industry. The challenge had evolved: we were no longer trying to start a business. Our goal was to achieve profitability by getting on the treadmill of reducing overhead and growing sales.

Back to the Future: The ECO

Although we had to take a 180° turn to get into business, my goal remained convincing employers to carve-out mental health and treat it as a free-standing benefit, much like dental. In furtherance of this goal, APM began to redeploy from selling primarily to HMOs as a subcapitator to selling directly to corporations. In 1987, I made what was one of my best decisions at APM. We exited the HMO business and concentrated exclusively on selling to employers. My concern with trying to do both simultaneously was that we would never build the service culture necessary to sell to corporations while operating in the price culture necessary to succeed in the HMO business. As a result of this decision, APM gave up about $9.5 million out of the $12 million in revenues that we had in 1986. Within two years, however, we had rebuilt the company to a larger revenue base, all from ECOs. We were finally ready for prime time.

The IBM Sale

The breakthrough sale that put APM on the map and established the ECO as a mainstream shelf product was IBM. In 1989 IBM was still the premier American corporation. When IBM issued an RFP for ECO proposals, everyone in the business salivated. Whoever closed the IBM contract would become the industry leader. In addition, there were likely to be many follow-on sales, since IBM represented the ultimate good housekeeping seal of approval. There was a great deal of drama associated with winning the IBM contract, but the two moments that stand out most in my mind were a catastrophe just before the RFP was due and IBM's announcement of the award. To write our final RFP response, key people within APM had drafted sections that were turned over for rewriting to a consulting firm that specialized in health care RFP's. Two days before the due date, I learned that we had a full-blown catastrophe on our hands. The consulting firm had lost whole sections of our response and had merged others into incomprehensible gibberish. Since it was too late to bring in another firm, I started a 36-hour solo marathon of rewriting the whole thing from start to stop. The finished product was not our best effort, but it was good enough to make APM one of only two finalists.

Then came the announcement of the award. The Chairman of IBM made a videotape that was shown simultaneously throughout the 50 states to 260,000 IBM employees. John Akers introduced the new managed behavioral health care program and then turned to IBM's benefits manager to announce the winner. IBM's domestic workforce was told that APM had been selected because IBM believed that APM was the best managed behavioral health care company in the business. That moment remains one of my proudest memories of the whole APM experience.

MOVING ON

In 1987, when I redeployed APM from an HMO to an employer-based company, it was necessary to recapitalize. We negotiated terms with a venture capital firm, but at the last second I accepted a somewhat less attractive offer from Value Health, Inc. (VHI). The major advantage of VHI was that, in the darkness of 1987, I doubted whether APM would get to the stage of having an Initial Public Offering (IPO) as a stand-alone company. Since I was looking for a retail exit strategy, I thought my best hope would be to have APM participate as part of another company's IPO. The strategy paid off on April 1, 1991, when VHI went public. As the third largest individual shareholder in VHI, I had a more than passing interest in the success of the IPO. The stock came out at 11 and began a steady climb to 60 before splitting three for two and climbing back to the high 50s. It was a heady experience, and a wonderful finale to my APM experience.

Nothing is forever, and knowing when to leave is a disappearing virtue. With VHI public, I had achieved my remaining goal within APM and gave notice that I would be leaving at the beginning of 1992. The APM experience had taken me from being a practicing psychiatrist to being the head of a company with more than 100 employees. My life had been changed in ways large and small. Looking back, I feel fortunate to have had the opportunity to be in the right place at the right time. For those readers thinking of taking the plunge, I can say that when it works, starting a business is about as good as it gets.

RECOMMENDED READING

Hastings, J. R. (1988), *Entrepreneurism and the Physician Executive.* Tampa, FL: American College of Physician Executives.

Lazarus, A. (1995), A business plan for starting a behavioral group practice. *Behavioral Healthcare Tomorrow*, 4(4):29–32.

Lifton, R. S. (1971), Protean man. *Arch. Gen. Psychiat.*, 24:298–304.

Index